The Naked Sommelier

A Laura McLove novel

CLAIRE DOYLE

CLAIRE DOYLE

Copyright © 2018 Claire Doyle

All rights reserved.

ISBN: 9781982907082

For all artists everywhere

Maybe it's better to arrive than travel hopelessly.

I first met Leo after my mother died. When the inheritance cheque arrived, I considered my options carefully and decided to visit a psychic.

Maggie Lightly advertised in the Evening Standard and I was not a little intrigued by where she lived: *she lived on Abbey Road.* She said her flat had a view of the zebra crossing.

Three days later, we sat at a table by her window and I gazed out at the street below. She spread the cards into a Celtic Cross.

"You're a writer," she said. I startled. She lifted my left hand, looked at the lifeline and said–damn her!–"You have the line of Mark Twain." I had never considered such a thing.

"Fiction or nonfiction?" I asked.

"What's the difference?" she replied. She was shrugging.

"One has a beginning, a middle and an end. The other is about facts …"

"What's the difference?" she said again.

I stared at her. I had nothing to say. I wasn't a writer. I didn't like writing and I didn't have a story. I looked out the window and thought about that album cover. It was *there*, that's where the fab four walked across the zebra crossing. People thought Paul McCartney was dead in 1969.

Who me? A writer? I followed her advice and wrote junk for a year and then I understood why writers shoot themselves, turn to drink and take off on road trips. I cursed that psychic. I'd only gone to see what her flat was like. *She lived on Abbey Road.*

Jobless, manless, childless and rudderless, I left London to add another to the list— homeless. Failure had been my towering achievement. Real life and its tick-tock lurked in the shadow but—like Morrissey—I'd never had a job because I never wanted one. There was one thing I now could do, however. I could afford to bugger off for a while. I fled London leaving the weary sense that everything in my life was over.Some go to Harvard, some go to Yale. Some go to Oxford or Cambridge. But I'm a mystic of a transcendentalist school.

Hell, I went to Emerson College.

1

Emerson College, Sussex, England, October 2009
It was a Friday morning and I heard the water outside my window. An odd sensation because I lived in the middle of the country, not by the sea. My window faced west from a tiny attic room with sloped roofing that I hit my head on as I opened it, and every morning someone—I never did find out who—switched on the garden water feature before I got up, and switched it off again in the late afternoon.

The sound of running water in the middle of the country was a pleasant sensation where there was no stream, and I imagined the air that came in the open window was energised with negative ions. I needed those energised ions. I had a hangover.

It was raining and, as it was a Friday, I skipped first class. We were reading Rudolf Steiner's *Agriculture Course* but it was unstudiable, incomprehensible, supersensible even, as they say here at Emerson, and I'd read it alone once during a long weekend and was none the wiser for my trouble. I sat on the armchair below the window, opened my journal and began to write.

I was forty-six then. Time was running out. Did I have enough of it left to write a novel? Jack Kerouac died at forty-seven from alcohol problems. I might just die with my novel inside me. I had learned about life and love but I couldn't get it to flow on the page. What did men write about? War. Women. Sex. The Big Issues. What did women write about? Men. Children. Love. That's what I decided to write about. Love. I opened my journal and began to write. Love. I wrote it again. Love. I deleted it. What is love? I deleted that too. What is sex? Ah! I began thinking about all the men I had ever known. Some nice. Some not so.

Men! Goddammit! The words weren't flowing, so what could I do? I needed a walk. I needed a holiday. What I had was a notebook and pen. I took my coat, hat, notebook and pen. I put on my boots and left the room. I walked down through Tablehurst farm, past the pigs, the Friday chicken slaughter and the heap of farm junk, on through mud past the apple orchard onto Forest Way and through the woods until the village green, but no-one was there as usual. Oh! Forest Row! You are too small for me! I wondered what to do with my day and as the sun was coming out, I took the bus to the seaside.

By midday I was on Brighton seafront. I bought a hot doughnut at the pier and began walking westwards in the direction of Hove. At least I was having a walk. I had my notebook. I had my pen. I was ready for action. I walked past the derelict West Pier as far as the Peace Angel and sat on a bench. I got out my notebook. I put my notebook back. I decided to walk back towards The Lanes and find a bookshop.

I found a bookshop. In the spiritual section, I picked up a book called a gratitude journal. Apparently by writing out what I wanted every day and feeling the sense of having it already, I could bring it to me. It was too good to be true! I could bring a novel to me! I could bring a man to me! I, Laura McLove will take on The Universe and I shall overcome! I bought the gratitude journal and went to the coffee shop. Now I had two notebooks and one pen. I found a copy of The Guardian, and ordered an Americano with milk. I sat on a sofa, opened the paper at the quick crossword and took out my pen.

The first clue was three across: 'pining for a loved one, (8)'. I wrote 'lovesick' across the boxes as my Americano arrived. I picked up two sugar lumps and plopped them in first, milk second, my spoon stirring last. I was happy. Was there ever a happier moment than a crossword and a coffee in a cafe all alone?

I had a poet friend years back. He spent his days walking and reading and drinking at art shows and we'd often sit in a cafe with a crossword. He didn't care which newspaper because he never bought one. He got annoyed when I was too quick filling in the answers only to get them wrong and make a mess of the thing. We idled many days together.

He recited a poem about me once at a poetry slam—'Laura The Tap Breaker'—about the day I broke a tap and the water was everywhere and I yelled at him, "You're useless!" when he couldn't help me fix it. He was only good for poetry and drinking. He'd adopted an aristocratic air, although he was from a council estate in Bermondsey. I also had an aristocratic disdain for work, the only decent thing the aristocracy ever gave us.

I was a walker, an idler, a fringe-dweller, a Gypsy and not quite yet but nearly—dare I?—a writer. What the hell was I doing studying biodynamic farming? It was so much *hard work*. I didn't want to be a farmer, I wanted to be a peasant.

One down: 'pining for a loved one, (8)'. I wrote 'lovelorn' down the boxes and across the previous entry. I finished up my coffee and left. Maybe today was a bad day for crosswords after all.

Returning through the village later, I came to the recycling centre. There was always something to find in here. I looked at the usual cast-offs and arrived at the bookshelf. I picked up an old paperback and read the whole first page. I was hooked. I had just struck gold in the village dump. The author? John Fante. I bought *Ask the Dust* for 20 pence and continued my way home.

There were students pruning apple trees in Tablehurst's orchard now. A French accent drew me up between the tree lines and I stopped in my tracks. "Hello. And what are you doing here pruning our English apple trees?"

"I'm learning biodynamics 'cos I'm gonna make wine back home," he said. "That's why I'm here." His beauty was astonishing. Eyes of cornflowers, hair of flax, lips for kissing. He was younger than me for sure. A beauty. A colt. A star in the night sky. And French. *Oh yes*. His name was Leo.

"I've never heard a French person say 'gonna' before–it's cute."

"Where are you from?" he asked.

"*Je suis Ecossaise*," I replied, "Scotland."

"You're accent is cute too, *c'est mignon*." He was beyond radiant and I was dazzled and wanting more but it would have to wait. For now, he had work. "I live in one of the attic rooms in the main building. They let me out once a day," I said as I walked away. "Come and knock on my door sometime." A French winemaker! Right on my doorstep! He'd got me from the first *merlot*.

Continuing home, I stood aside for the John Deere tractor to pass and at the top of the hill I turned to see the forest once more with its rain-soaked, blue-green hue. It was stunning. Past the second apple orchard and horses on my right, down another little hill and there's the pond and uphill again onto Emerson campus until I stood bang in the middle in front of reception. There she was to meet me. Lilly, my one and only friend in the world, all a-blonde and ginger sitting by the puddle. Lilly the college cat.

Lilly was a free range being. Outcast from her former home as there was a new baby in the house, she had found her way up to the attic and so I took her in and fed her. She was very welcome to my little room and was often camped outside the door when I came home. Me and Lilly managed our lives quietly. She was too wet to pick up that day so I let her follow me indoors and up the stairs until we reached the top. I gave her a rub down with a towel and let her settle on the bed. She began purring and cleaning herself and went to sleep.

I lay down next to her and thought about writing but didn't. One day I would write, but that day wasn't today. Every day might be that day but somehow that day never became today. The days of waiting were upon me. The days in which nothing very much happened. The days when I didn't seem to make very much happen. Oh boredom! Walking, writing, coffee, thinking, dreaming of another day when things would happen. I opened the John Fante novel. It was about a young man struggling to be a writer.

2

On Brighton Pier in a dream, the pier sparkling with fairy lights. A happy feeling with fairground music playing. All at once I was standing on my mother's grave. Still a happy feeling. A scroll on the grave revealed a word: 'pregnancy'. There was a white bird in front of me now, a dove I supposed. The bird split in two as I picked it up becoming an object rather than a living bird now and embarrassed, I placed the broken bird on the grave in two pieces with the thought that I would return to mend it later.

      I woke and wondered if I could be pregnant. It was impossible. I got my pen out. I counted up the years I had been coupled. I was thirty years into adulthood, just five years I'd been officially coupled and adding up the long tail-ending of love affairs and the affairs that didn't work out I could take that to ten years. Twenty years single. That was a lot of acting interested, as Jerry Seinfeld once said. It was also a lot of not having sex to deal with. No wonder I was exhausted—and sexually frustrated. I needed a haircut. That would make me feel better. I needed a man. Maybe like a hole in the head or like a fish needs a bicycle but God! Give me something! I was a seething cauldron of frustration but you would never know it to look at me. Make love, McLove! It's your name stupid! It's what you're supposed to do! Do it! Do something!

3

It was a few days before I met Leo again. It was raining so I couldn't go for my usual walk, my counterpoint to writing or, in my case, not writing. So this particular day found me in the college library. I decided to bring Lilly with me. She didn't like the rain much either, being a cat.

An overwhelming odour of old books pervaded the room and I mean *old*. There was an original copy of Madame Blavatsky's *The Secret Doctrine* and that other old classic, Dion Fortune's *Psychic Self Defence*. The room had the feel of an occultist's library which, in fact, it was. It had a still and heavy sense and and there was a floor creak from time to time although the verdant surroundings outside pressed in with the light through the high windows.

On the few occasions the librarian was in, you could see books and index cards on her desk piled as high as her bouffant hair and she was surely the only person who understood the borrowing system. She had probably read *Psychic Self Defence*. She had probably understood it. She spoke with a posh English accent. Someone told me she was ninety years old.

The library had the only campus wireless connection. A Danish student had said he could sense electromagnetic fields and had conducted a full college campaign to disallow its use. He won in the end—except for the library—but left the college as he upset so many people in the process but mainly he upset himself.

Such was life at Emerson—one foot in the modern world and one foot firmly entrenched in the deep, occult past. Yes, Emerson College was a Mystery School. I was lying on the sofa, shoes off, with my back to the high window reading *The Prime Of Miss Jean Brodie*. At least I hadn't been sent to an all-girls school as a child, I thought, although I did spend a year being taught by an Irish nun.

I looked up when I heard the door open. I saw an angel. It was Leo. He broke into a smile and I was sunk and I knew it.

"Is that your cat?" he asked in that gorgeous French voice. Lilly was purring on my lap.

"I've adopted her whilst she's here," I said. "She belongs to Francis in fact, but the new baby means it's difficult in the house so, well the truth is, I think she's adopted me. You know what cats are like. Her name is Lilly."

"I like cats," he said. He sat down next to me on the sofa. I sensed his aroma, the smell of his sweater, his shampoo, the rain on him.

"What have you come in for?" I asked.

"I'm looking for the wine directory. D'you know where it is? I haven't used the library much so far." I pointed to the agriculture section.

"So tell me about wine," I said.

"It's made from grapes," he replied. I laughed.

"Tell me about you. Tell me about you and wine!"

"I'm a *sommelier*."

"How exciting!"

"Yeah, I know all about wine. I worked at The Dorchester once. I was the head wine waiter."

"Head *sommelier* at The Dorchester. You must have served some famous people."

"Yeah, Paul McCartney …"

"God, I love Paul McCartney! What did he drink?"

"He drank a *Château Haut Brion 1989*."

"Any other Beatles?"

"What do you mean?"

"Did you serve any other Beatles? You know, Ringo Starr, George Harrison?"

"No, I didn't. But I served Madonna once."

"God! I love Madonna! What did she drink?"

"Very expensive mineral water!" he said. "I used to work for Gordon Ramsay too."

"Was he hard to work for?"

"All kitchens are tough and hard work, it's just the way it is." He got up from the sofa and went in the direction of the wine directory. I liked his arse. "I've found it!" He returned to the sofa. I liked his thighs.

"I wanna make my own wine," he said. He held the book up to show me. "This lists all the biodynamic winemakers in the world. There's loads of them in France but most keep quiet about it because they'd be seen as mad. I wanna make a natural wine, you know, without chemicals, and using the yeast in the air and on the surface of the grapes, farm with horses, low impact, no additives."

"Can you really do that these days?"

"The real good wine comes from a mixed farm with a vineyard. You won't find it for sale much anywhere, it sells privately. My parents have a farm back in Bordeaux. I remember when they had horses but now it's all tractors. Do you like wine?" he asked.

"I love wine. Back in London, I hung out with a bunch of artists and poets, freeloaders, big drinking intellectual types and we would go around together in the east end to all the art openings for free drinks. I even learnt something about art. They didn't seem to mind me hanging on to them, I don't think they gave a shit."

"I love the east end," he said.

"Where are you going to work next summer?" All farming students took work placements on a farm. "I dunno," he replied. "I gotta bad knee so I don't know if I can do too much real heavy work. I'm thinking of north America."

I could go on about our first conversation, a getting to know you thing, but here's what you need to know—Leo was a traveller and so was I. He was an expert in something with which I had a longstanding, complicated relationship—wine. He knew how to make it, he was here to learn how to do it *au naturel*. He was a man of the earth. He was a man of the *terroir*. And he was hot. Hot. HOT. The only men for me are the traveller men and Leo for me will always be the Traveller Man. I was an amateur at love and I was about to learn that I needed to go pro.

Back in the attic later, I tried to remember it all. I was in a deep hypnosis. My mind and hormones had gone into overdrive. Lilly meowed at my feet but I couldn't think straight to feed her. I had to work something out. How on earth did that gorgeous man get here into this college on his own and still be single? It defied the laws of the Universe. Or did it? I picked up that gratitude journal I bought in Brighton. I picked up my pen. And I wrote.

"I am so happy and grateful Leo and I are spending next summer together and are in love."

It was done. It was on its way. It was all I had to do so I wrote it again.

"I am so happy and grateful Leo and I are spending next summer together and are in love."

I laughed aloud then went to the kitchen to find Lilly's crunchies. I filled her water bowl and her crunchie bowl and she sat munching and crunching on the floor by the door. She had no idea of the spiritual forces I was bringing to bear for us in our little room. She was a cat and I loved her.

I picked up my violin from the bed. It was flawed—I had made it myself—and I'd varnished it a burnt orange colour like my hair. It took me eighteen months to persevere and finish and I'd decorated it with a ruby ribbon around the scroll. A classical musician wouldn't say so—they're hard to please aren't they?—but my one violin was more beautiful than all the violins in all the world because I had made it. I hung it back onto the wall where it lived. I'd placed my name tab inside the soundbox on the wrong side before I glued it over. I was useless at detail but I was good at the bigger picture and I was good at imagining things—like me and Leo in bed. In love. On holiday.

I poured myself a glass of Romanian pinot noir, just one glass, and I turned on my iPlayer. Barry! Yes Barry Manilow,

Could It Be Magic? Was there a better pop song ever written? I fell deeper into my reverie. A cyclone was whirling in my mind.

4

The following morning I began a new routine. I had coffee as usual—this one from an Indian elephant farm—brewed it in a little Italian coffee pot, then drank it from my red mug with white dots, together with one tablespoon of single cream and one demerara sugar. I sat on my chair and opened the gratitude journal. I relished moments like this at the beginning of the day.

"I am so happy and grateful that Leo and I are spending next summer together and are in love."

What did that mean? How would that feel? It seemed ridiculous right now but I cleansed my mind of those thoughts. I was so much older than him, how would that work? He was French of course and French men like older women. I started to wonder what kind of woman Leo would be attracted to. What kind of woman would I need to be to draw him in? I pondered all the actresses I admired, for their acting, intelligence, beauty and general fabulousness until I settled on one and I knew she was the right one: Sharon!

I settled on Sharon Stone.

"I am so happy and grateful now that I am as beautiful and fabulous as Sharon Stone!"

How I laughed! Lilly opened her eyes and stretched out her right paw and yawned. She stood up and arched her back to waken herself. Lilly loved her body.

In retrospect, after the motherf*cker of a trip, I wondered whether the problem wasn't simply a question of sentence structure—if I had written "I am so happy and grateful now that Leo and I are in love and spending our summer together"—would there have been a different outcome? Could everything be this simple? Well, of course, it could.

Sadly, it wasn't.

Was I happy? Was I grateful? Hell, no. This is what needed to change. What would Sharon do? Sharon would have a personal trainer, a protein diet, a spiritual counsellor, and zillions in the bank. I could make a start. I could do with losing half a stone. Action stations! I resolved to join the local gym. The thought then came to me—what would Lilly do? I laughed aloud once more. My beautiful pussy cat could teach me a thing or two.

Just then there was a knock on my door. Leo? Alas, it wasn't but no matter, it was Delphine. My life was manifesting a lot of French people right now. She lived in the next attic room, a farmer's daughter from Cathar country, south-west France. I took my hat off to Delphine. She had once killed a chicken with her own bare hands. I told her of my plans.

"So this is my plan, Delphine. I've got carte blanche come Easter to do what I want. What I want is to travel and I want to be with Leo. I'm asking the Universe to let us spend our summer together. In the meantime, I've got to get into his league."

"How are you going to do that?" she asked.

"I'm going to draw him in with the law of attraction. He is going to ask me to spend the summer with him. I won't have to push at all," I said. "That's how it's supposed to work anyhow."

"Good luck Laura. I think you might need it," said Delphine. "You are always welcome at our place, you know."

I got dressed in my best outfit—remembering Sharon—and went to class. I took Lilly outside and let her go for the day. I still hadn't written anything but I felt that my life might at last be moving.

5

We were an international group of farmers that year. Half of us were young and half of us were middle aged. Half of us were men and half of us weren't. It made for a healthy and combustible mix.

Today we were studying earth energy. A Swiss farmer called Dieter, complete in national dress, was taking us around the campus. He rocked the place. He had smoked marijuana once, he said, and it had opened his mind to other realms. From that day onwards, he resolved to expand his consciousness without drugs. He recommended *How to Know Higher Worlds* by Rudolf Steiner as a handbook for farmers. He had a long, long beard and had training in a counselling that involved exploring past lives and helped young people who had lost their way at his horse farm in Switzerland. We walked to to the top of the vegetable garden together towards the compost heaps.

Biodynamics was a journey and couldn't be learnt extrinsically. It was practically inexplicable, it seemed to involve everything. It was a crazy wisdom. You didn't have to believe in it necessarily, but you did need to experience. You had to allow yourself to be changed by it—to put your inner being in the compost, so to speak. In shorthand, it was all about the moon. Wherever the moon is on its journey each month through the twelve constellations of the zodiac, dictates whether it is a good day for sowing, transplanting or harvesting. An old German woman had come up with an almanac, dividing the moon's cycle into days that were fruit, flower, leaf or root as a quick ready reckoner for the astronomically challenged. Today the moon was in Aries, making it a fruit day.

We stood around the first compost heap and Dieter asked us, "How does the compost feel to you? Does it feel hot? Or cold? Warm? How does it feel?"

I stood with my back straight and centred myself. I felt my inner body and located myself at my solar plexus and tried to feel the compost heap. It was cold. The compost was fully matured and it had no energy. We could all sense it. We moved to another compost heap. "How does this one feel? Active? Hot? How does it feel?" said Dieter. This time the answer was "warm". The compost heap was still active and breaking down.

We moved on to the flower garden where there were heaps of leaf mold. "How does it feel?" asked Dieter, once more. The answer came again. The leaf mold was cold. It didn't look fully matured—maybe it had become inactive and needed some extra carbon or nitrogen matter.

The leaves came from the autumn leaf-raking that all students took part in and was a good weeding process in itself as you could see who was capable of physical work or not. Surprisingly, a few gardening and farming students weren't quite up to it. I was up to it but only in fits and starts as befits someone who wouldn't want a full-time farmer's life, maybe more like a full-time farmer's wife.

I brought an image of Leo up into my mind's eye, I centred on my solar plexus and tried to see how he felt. The answer came—he was warm. He generated a genuine human warmth, someone who liked other human beings. He was also hot but that feeling was coming from my root chakra. The sexual one.

We were often taken around the grounds on teaching missions to study earth energy. We would be asked to stand in a circle, hold hands and imagine a white protective light surrounding us then attempt to sense how the energy flowed. At times, it was a simple matter to see where the animals gathered or where clutter was dumped. There was often a ton of stuff dumped on big farms. Too many men, not enough flowers would be my usual diagnosis. I enjoyed these classes but drew the line when we were holding hands and asked to sing together. It was an insult to music.

The previous summer, I had gone to study huge mustard plants in a polytunnel late in the afternoon when the sun was at its most intense. I stared and stared at those mustard plants from every angle for a week—they were *huge*—and sure enough, one night, I had a dream of huge leafy plants but I couldn't discern any meaning to the dream. I just hadn't cut the mustard.

I'd camped out that July at the top of the vegetable garden and I would hear the owls twit-twoo at night and the Tablehurst Sussex Browns lowing and shuffling in the darkness in the neighbouring field. I awoke every morning to a line of bright yellow sunflowers and blue cornflowers on my sight horizon before the vegetable terraces slipped down the hill. I tasted raw corn in the morning fresh off the stalk for the first time, sweet and yellow. The gardener was growing the three sisters of squash, corn and beans— companion plants that blossomed together.

I was also one of three sisters. It had taken a lifetime to realise I could never blossom with them around. I often felt out of sync with the world, as if I was prey. It wasn't the more-than-human world I was afraid of, you understand, it was low grade human beings that frightened me. I didn't find them phony exactly, I thought of them as *matterheads*. The ones who think that the physical world is all there is. The trouble with them is this though— being outer directed and terrified of failure, they need a scapegoat. So what if you're a woman, black, poor, Gypsy even, what if you're the talented one, or the one who worked so hard to achieve balance? Those *matterheads* would get you in the end. Worse, now no-one would get the prize. A *matterhead* aims for lose-lose. It would be true to say that no-one at Emerson was a *matterhead*. I had found my tribe even if some of them seemed as if they had orbited the planet a few times.

I had discovered a bathroom upstairs in the main building during my summertime camp and I sneaked in and had a hot bath once in awhile because no-one was paying attention. There was a philosophy of freedom here. Freedom to be yourself, to lie to yourself, to turn up to class or not, to turn up late if you wished, no discipline, nobody to blame—a bit Zen, really. Some students had studied for a whole three years including room and board and hadn't paid a thing and then there was the boomerang effect. People came back again and again over the years to study one subject after another, even—Godforbid—clowning. So, like Hotel California, you might never leave. I now realise why—the real world is hell.

      My day took a regular rhythm that summer. I got up at seven and dressed outside my tent, only once having a rambler pass by as I pulled my knickers up one morning. I would see the geese fly over towards the reservoir and make my way indoors to breakfast. We started work at 8 am, twice a week harvesting vegetables for the kitchen, other times planting, weeding and watering. After lunch it was more of the same until a tea break and then stopping at 5 pm. I would nip into the main building again to wash or do a laundry and sometimes I would wander down to the village. I would see—and hear—the geese fly back from the reservoir in the evening in their geese-shaped arrow high above me in the sky.

6

Later that day I was back in my room with Lilly. The phone rang. It was Delphine. She was at the pizza place in the village and asked me to join her. I forgot I was going on a diet for a moment and decided to go out. I left Lilly in my room asleep.

I walked my usual walk to the village although this time when I passed the gym, I went right in and joined then and there and walked out again. I took a shortcut on the path by the business centre, past the bakery then the red post box, up a little steep incline to the village hall. I took a right to *Java and Jazz* and Delphine. I loved Delphine. She was beautiful and clever and sensible. She didn't have any characteristics that silly women everywhere seemed to have, the kind that I had. She was still a woman though and not without class. Sharon would approve of her. I approved of her. I wished I could be a bit more like her.

We ordered a margherita pizza each and a bottle of Italian red *Cuvée Monferrato* between us. I wondered why she had wanted to see me. "Why did you want to see me?" I asked.

"No reason. I thought it might be fun."

"Do you know anything about Leo?" I enquired. "Come on! You've got gossip!"

"You've got competition!"

"As if I didn't know! I'm taking the long road, via stealth," I replied.

"The whole college is after him. I can't believe it. I mean, I'm French too so he doesn't have the same effect on me. He is very good-looking though!"

"Oh don't tell me you want him too!"

"No! He's not for me! I want you to have him. But all these women in their twenties are going crazy for him! They follow him around the place!"

"I know, I've seen it." Our wine arrived and I poured us both a glass.

"*Santé!*"

"Cheers, my dear!" We clinked, sipped and huddled towards each other again.

"This wine's a knockout," I said, twirling the neck of my glass on the table.

"There's two of them! Andrea and Suzanne! They talk about him all the time! They're nuts for him! They look so stupid!"

"He can't be taken in by it surely?"

"I don't know. Men don't think the way we do, they don't see it," she said.

"I know. At least there's pizza," I said, tearing into mine. "But I've got a weapon. The law of attraction. I swear I'll make it work if it's the last thing I do."

"He has a woman!"

"No! Who? Where?"

"In Canada! He fell for her completely. It turns out he only knew her for two days in a youth hostel or something. She's a lawyer. She went travelling for a year after college and now she's settled back in Canada."

"So that's why he wants to go to north America," I mused. I tore off a piece of pizza and began to eat. This law of attraction stuff was way more complicated than I thought.

"Did they have an affair?" I asked her.

"No, they didn't. He's just nuts about her, that's all."

"After two days?"

"Well, how long did it take you to fall for him?"

"*Touché*. Point taken. Drat. When we finish here, shall we go to the pub for a swift half?" I felt like getting drunk.

"Let's see how it goes … this pizza is good and the wine, as you say, is a knockout."

"Tell me your other news, Delphine. Cheer me up—how come you know all this anyhow?" I said.

"Everyone knows all this. My mother says you can come to our farm next summer. I've told her all about you. They love having visitors and she speaks good English," she said.

"I have a Plan B! Thank your mother very much. I'd love to visit," I said. "Is there anyone you like at college?"

"No, I've had enough of men for now," she replied. "I'll be on the farm next summer too and I'd love you to come. Maybe I can find a job in France, or anywhere for that matter." We ate up our pizza and finished the wine. Delphine liked to drink too and, as she was French, she remained a keen smoker.

We stopped at the Foresters for a nightcap.

"I'm depressed," I said. "Bloody men. Bloody women. I've decided to take Sharon Stone as my role model. Do you have a role model?" I asked Delphine.

"No, I've never thought about it."

"Every time I'm in a predicament I ask myself this question—what would Sharon do? and wait for the answer."

"What would Sharon do in the predicament you're in now?" she asked.

"Bloody Sharon Stone is so bloody gorgeous that no man could look anywhere else. However, bloody Sharon Stone wouldn't bloody give up now, would she? So neither will I. And that's final."

7

"I am so happy and grateful now that Leo and I are spending our summer together and are in love."

I awoke early the next morning, turfed Lilly off the bed and headed straight for my gratitude journal. I was in a surprisingly good mood, despite the previous evening's revelations. It had been a good night out with Delphine. We had been so drunk we talked in French on the way home and I had barely understood a word. And I had an invitation to *Bellelavie*, the family farm, next summer if my Plan A didn't work out. Things were looking up.

I got back to my Plan A. What would Sharon do? Best foot forward was my guess. I switched on Barry Manilow again, put on my best jeans, purple fitted sweater and tied my hair up. I applied just a little cover-up and blusher and spritzed a spritz of *eau de fleur*. I skipped the first class due to last night's dehydration but I climbed downstairs with Lilly to join everyone for the 10 o'clock coffee break. I was as fabulous as Sharon Stone.

The main lobby had dark oak floors and wall panelling with a portrait of college namesake Ralph Waldo Emerson above the staircase. The ceilings were high and the walls were cream where the panelling stopped. The dining rooms—there were three of them on the ground floor—never lost the ooze of a million communal meals absorbed over the years despite doors and windows frequently opened for air.

The college coffee was never as good as my own. Nobody's coffee was as good as my own. I made mine with single cream and there wasn't a new fangled American or Italian style coffee place for miles that made coffee with cream. It was skinny this and that, double whipped cream with sprinkles on top, marshmallows, disgusting flavoured syrups. I could start my own coffee shop—simply filtered or brewed, just add cream. College coffee was filtered fair-trade organic from a women's co-operative in Bolivia. A delicate aroma of oestrogen, just add milk. It would have to do.

    I saw Leo. He was a spiritual man but he had two attachments—Andrea and Suzanne. I smiled a 'hello' and nodded and left him to it.

    Welcome to the Emerson Bubble. If you could handle the dogma—and the lack of men—it was a good place to live. It isn't only a college you see, it's also a community. A relic from those revolutionary days of the sixties of which I was a child.

    I had never wanted money or property so I hadn't done the things you have to do to get them. I had never wanted marriage or children. I was a lost generation in a way, all to myself, but there wasn't anything wrong with me. Far from it, it was everything around me that had changed. I hadn't shot John Lennon, I hadn't created MTV, I hadn't told Dylan go get born again. I was beat, sure, but beat as in beatific. I was sometimes down but never out.

    And then there was the Emerson architecture.

    Everything had a slope—the roofs, the windows, the windows on the doors. The student houses looked like hobbit homes only bigger. They were named after trees. Oaktree. Birch. Maple.

    I shouldn't have been studying farming—I had no real interest in it at all. I was interested in learning to grow my own food or at least having the skills. I could stay away from the real world if I had those skills, a world as far away from London and stupid modern people as I could get with plenty of time to write, or not write, as seemed to be the case in my new so-called post carbon life. Living in a city was a humiliating experience. Why had I put up with it? Because I knew of nothing else. I had been living in its seamless hologram.

    And the beauty of Emerson was, well, the beauty of Emerson.

    I left the building to sit outside with the smokers. I took another sip of coffee and said to myself:

"I am so happy and grateful now that Leo and I are travelling together next summer and are in love."

Later that afternoon I made my first visit to the gym.

8

One Saturday morning I awoke wildly early–an effect of drinking Muscadet the night before - and I collected the college newspapers from the post box. I wasn't so fussed on the *International Herald Tribune* but I was fussed on *The Guardian* with the quick crossword. I sat in the common room on the ground floor, enjoying the late autumn sun streaming through the windows and opened the Review section. Who should walk in but Leo? The Universe was delivering! He looked alluring, dishevelled from getting out of bed, or so my feverish imagination told me.

"What you up to this morning?" I asked.

"I don't know what to do with myself, I woke early. I can't meditate any longer." He flopped himself onto the sofa and there was Lilly following him through the door.

"I thought the point of meditation was to get you at peace with yourself."

"It doesn't cure everything."

"Stroke the cat, it might help." Lilly had jumped onto his lap. "Do you use a mantra?"

"I love you." He gave me a wide grin and Lilly began purring loudly.

"I love you too."

"It's my mantra. I love you. I say it to everything."

"Including me." I smiled.

"I say it to God. I got it from an old Hawaiian guy when I was in India."

"What was a Hawaiian guy doing in India doling out mantras, pray?"

"We were staying at the same ashram. He told me a lot about Hawaii and said it was a good mantra and it stuck."

"You say, '*je t'aime*' though, right?"

"Yeah I say *je t'aime*." He was laughing now. "I know it sounds stupid but it works. Any mantra works. How could that one not work?"

"I think the only words I know in different languages are 'two beers please?' I wonder what the Divine would say if I offered that as a prayer?"

"*Deux bières s'il vous plaît*! At least you'd make him laugh," he said, shaking his head. "Why are you up so early?"

"Just one of those things. I like to snatch *The Guardian* before anyone else does. I'm obsessed with the quick crossword. I've been doing it for years. Maybe it's my meditation."

We were quiet for a moment as he cuddled Lilly and I stared at the newspaper and turned a page. The only sound was Lilly purring.

"I couldn't settle in France after all that travelling. I wonder if I'll ever be able to stay in one place?" he said, breaking the silence.

"Take it as a sign you're still alive. We were nomads a lot longer than we've been settled, you know. Some people can't imagine life outside of an office, a mortgage and coupledom. Some people think it's an achievement to get a mortgage! An achievement to be in debt to a bank! And look what a mess the banks have got us in."

"In French, *mortgage* means death pledge."

"God forbid. You're more alive than other people, that's all. You've not been totally domesticated. Neither have I, for that matter. The restlessness means you're alive, that's why you like to travel. Either that, or it's plain old sexual frustration. Either way, it means you're alive and not dead. And that's surely a good thing?"

"That makes me feel better!"

"Settled agriculture was the beginning of the problem if you think about it, and I have thought about it. At length."

"Yeah, vines are wild and have to be cultivated."

"The wild must be tamed and controlled."

"You mean wine?"

"Well it helps. Civilisation needs something to survive it and wine's as civilised as it gets—in a good way."

"I really wanna make my wine one day."

"I really wanna drink it."

"I just gotta figure out how to travel and do the wine thing too. You can't tend vines if you're always moving. You can't be with the grapes when they're growing, then harvesting, then fermenting and all the rest."

"Then move slow. When the oil finally runs out, you'll have to anyway."

"When the oil runs out, people will need my wine because I'll know how to make it naturally and I won't be using oil."

"And that's your answer. Travel 'til the oil runs out. The very act of your travelling will bring the moment closer 'cos you'll be using up resources, it's a perfect plan."

"So there's nothing to worry about."

"*Rien à faire*. Nothing to do and nothing to worry about."

9

The days continued. The sun shone, the rain fell, the water feature trickled its soothing sound in the background, Lilly went out to wander and Lilly came back again. I went to classes. I tried to write, I thought about Leo, I took long walks. I wrote out my gratitude journal. I didn't go out of my way to try to find him because The Universe would drop him in my lap again, I felt sure.

I read the John Fante novel in astonishment. Such a lightness of touch. He made it all seem so easy. Lilly watched me read with her two lovely eyes. All the time I wanted to write a novel, and I wrote precisely NOTHING. I went for walks, the same walk, the same old walk I walked like other people one hour there, one hour back on the Forest Way to mediocre East Grinstead two or three times a week. I figured it would help with my weight, and balance up the drinking. People thought I walked as some kind of nature trail, or some kind of spiritual practice, but I walked in the same way as Bukowski went to the races—it was something at the other end of the stick to writing, or in my case, not writing.

There was writing and there was not writing. Hemingway had bullfights, Bukowski had the races, I had walking. Walk, walk, walk. I never walked around the place and I never thought about it, I walked the Forest Way to East Grinstead and back over and over to get my mind to shut up. I had to siphon off the energy. I was trying to cut through, to stay sane, to live in nothing and maybe when I returned I would write something. More usual what would happen is I would lie on my bed once more and think about writing. And then I would read awhile, maybe I would play Classic FM on my computer—a way to avoid thinking about music—and then I would cook and eat and open some wine and another day would pass. I wasn't accumulating pages but I would get up off my bed once in a while and write something in a burst of inspiration. It never added up to much. On the other hand, I seemed to be acquiring a taste for Vivaldi.

I thought about taking them on, you know, the Bukowskis, the Ginsbergs, the Scott Fitzgeralds—no, maybe not Scott F—but the Bukowskis and the Ginsbergs I could have a shot at, I understood them. There was something else I knew about, more than Bukowski, I knew about music. I knew what it meant to be an artist in today's money-making world.

So maybe I should take them on? I could vent my literary gender dysmorphia. I could do a Knut Hamsun and write a novel about nothing in particular. That was it! Nothing in particular! I could write about myself and being a writer! Genius! Why didn't I think of it before! I knew I was on track. I lifted myself up off my bed along with Lilly and went for a walk. I left Lilly at the door. I had walking and I had wine, I had writing. Halfway through my walk I wondered whether taking long soaks in the bath wouldn't be better for my knees. I needed writing, goddammit write something!

10

After showering one morning, I noticed a tiny growth on my left breast. It had been there a while but hadn't caught my attention like it did that day. It was ugly. With the thought in mind that Leo would definitely come my way because of the universal forces I was bringing to bear, I realised that I'd rather live without it, this little tag of skin that occupied an important part of my body. I asked myself, what would Sharon do? And the answer came—surgery.

I went to the doctor. He said, there's a specialist who comes in once a week, come in on Friday at 9am.

Friday at 9am I found myself waiting in the Forest Row doctors' surgery and who would walk in? Yes! Leo! And on his own!

"Hi Laura, how are you?"

"Hey Leo! I'm good. Fancy meeting you here. I hope you're OK?"

"I'm OK. I'm gonna get my knee seen to. A doctor in France told me years ago I should get it operated on before I'm thirty. I'm twenty-nine now so I thought it was time." I noticed he was holding a mobile phone. "I got myself a phone at last. You should give me your number." So I did.

"Text me so I have yours too," I said, as I was called into the doctor's office.

The lovely skin specialist took pity on me and my little nick of skin in such a delicate place and said he would remove it. I lay down on the table and he injected a needle into my breast. My breast was having an anaesthetic. He then took a knife and cut the little thing off and placed paper stitches over the cut. He said to not go to the gym for a week until it had healed. I thanked him and left the surgery a new woman. Leo had already gone but my self-esteem was shooting up. I switched on my phone. I had a text from Leo! "Bonjour Mademoiselle Laura. Leo." I was ecstatic.

    I headed back to my room, fed Lilly as usual, and wrote up an entire essay on dairy that I'd been putting off. I was still listening to *Could It Be Magic?* and then I remembered—somebody brilliant found a disco version in *Could It Be Magic?* and that person was Donna Summer. I downloaded an mp3 file from the internet and danced around the room. So much better than Barry. A memory of rainy caravan holidays in Scotland came to mind, eating morning rolls with orange cheese and listening to Radio One, wondering when the rain would ever end.

    I had my first glass of verdejo that evening, a Spanish white wine from La Mancha.

11

I was getting cold in my single bed. The temperature was beginning to drop and I was sleeping under a couple of duvets in an old sweater and socks and still the central heating couldn't come on early enough. Even Lilly could feel the chill. The attic was so quiet.

I looked out the kitchen window as my coffee brewed and saw the Sussex Brown herd out there and a whole lot of tranquility descended on me. And just think! I could be rushing to an office and getting some kids up! There was a certain emptiness being alone in your forties. I had learned to maximise its use, however, and had developed a pretty good relationship with myself over the years and nurtured times alone. It wasn't that I didn't need anybody—I did. I liked knowing there were people around but I didn't necessarily want to talk to any of them. The one I wanted to talk to was proving a tad difficult to access. It reminded me of that old Carpenters' song *Close To You*—every woman in the place wanted to be next to Leo. How to get close without anyone noticing my strategy? There were beady, jealous eyes everywhere and like any good predator, I wanted to act alone.

I returned to Lilly in my room with my morning coffee and got going with the gratitude thing. Maybe I could just ask him out?

And still the writing wasn't coming. I still had a wine habit but I was keeping it in line with the fitness programme. I had a gym habit, a wine habit, a walking habit. At least I'd written my dairy essay, that was progress.

I decided to experiment with Bukowski's method and let the 'typer' do the work. Music, booze and the writing would do itself. I visited the village dump that day and found two chipped champagne glasses for 25p each. I bought a bottle of cava, the Spanish sparkling wine and played Classic FM, Prokofiev's Romeo and Juliet. It tasted great but it didn't work. Two nights later I tried Italian prosecco, and listened to Mantovani but that didn't work either. Another day, I bought *vin mousseux*—it was disgusting—and found French rap on the internet. I liked the rap so much I got over involved with it and still the words wouldn't come. I was becoming a drunk. Strangely though, the walking, the gym and the general physical work of learning farming and gardening was removing the weight anyhow. I realised something else about myself too—I had become a loner. I realised I had been this way for a long time.

12

It was a cold night, the night of the Christmas booze up. Anyone and everyone was going to the Chequers Inn. I met Leo in the college laundry and made sure he knew the details. I showered and lathered and dressed as fabulously as Sharon Stone.

I arrived early and sat on a bench by the window opposite Delphine. I was settling in when Leo came in and, like a miracle, he came around the table and sat beside me.

"Would you like a drink *mesdemoiselles* Laura and Delphine?"

"Yes." We replied in unison.

"Guinness for me, probably Guinness for you too, no?" I looked at Delphine.

"Yeah I'll have a Guinness too."

Leo went to the bar, ordered the drinks and sat down.

"So how are things with you, Leo? When are you going back to France for Christmas?" I asked.

"Tomorrow on the Eurostar. I'm not looking forward to it much. I've got the knee operation before Christmas."

"Oh, poor you. I'll be thinking of you," I said. "How did you damage your knee in the first place?"

"Football."

"You don't seem like the kind of guy who's into *le futbol*," I said.

"Not anymore I'm not. I was before I got into wine."

"Have you decided on where you'll be working next summer?" asked Delphine. She was steering the conversation. Good old Delphine.

"I bought a return ticket to Canada from France," he said. "I'll be leaving college at Easter so I'll be back in France again for a while beforehand."

"How come Canada?" I asked, dreading the answer. Delphine and I exchanged a glance.

"I've got a friend there I'd like to see and there's a farm near her in Toronto. They've agreed to take me on for a few weeks so that's my plan." My heart sank. I was feeling about as fabulous as six feet under. "How about you Laura? You're finishing aren't you?" he said.

"Yeah, I think I'm going to spend my summer with Delphine at her parents' place. I've got an open invitation. After that, I dunno," I replied.

"My mother's going to love you," said Delphine. I wished somebody would, I thought.

"I'd like to come and see your farm sometime too," said Leo. My spirits lifted for a moment and then I thought maybe he likes Delphine? I was confused. I took another sip of Guinness. Delphine's place did sound amazing. Her parents had farmed biodynamically for forty years and they had a vineyard too. They sold at the market in Cahors and produced a piece of black magic, a black wine, *Clos de Bellelavie*. I was looking forward to it, my summer in the southwest but it seemed like it would be without the sparkling angel creature, Leo.

I took another sip. I loved Guinness in an authentic Guinness glass. Leo was drinking it too. Suzanne and Andrea arrived but with Delphine as my threshold guardian, they would have to go elsewhere. At least I wouldn't have to spend my summer with them, I thought. The pub was filling and even tutors showed up along with a few farmers from Tablehurst. Emerson types were none too keen on alcohol in the main because it interfered with your consciousness–which was exactly why I liked it. Who needs reality when a pint of Guinness beckons, especially with a packet of salt 'n' vinegar crisps? Some of my most spiritual moments have been when I've lain in bed alone with a hangover.

No to alcohol but yes to meat–it was a curious set of beliefs. The peasant farmer of Austro-Hungary inspired the biodynamic view on the world, as well as a whole bunch of Hindu thinking–reincarnation, karma, etheric bodies, astral bodies. It involved the sun and the moon and the stars, the heavens, everything visible and invisible, the karma of the earth through birth and rebirth. No wonder it was ignored by scientists. On the other hand, what did they know about lived experience? They had undermined consciousness, therefore love. Dead matter couldn't process meaning, I could. I had been as intrepid as Columbus on my inner journey.

Scientists taught us man was alone in the universe but only a man could think up that one. Woman wasn't alone, she was part of a thinking, breathing, fucking, giant *feeling*. I was the centre of it and as the Universe was infinite, or Infinite, everyone else was the centre of it too, they just wouldn't be the centre of mine. Yes, scientific materialism had left the Emerson buildings, cartesian rationalism an idea whose time had come and long gone and I lived up in the attic on a probability wave, the probability of what remained to be seen.

We trotted round en masse to The Foresters which had a late licence and I watched Leo play pool. He reminded me of my younger self. It made me feel like I was back in my twenties again, hanging around late at night for a bloke I'd like to fall into my lap so I fled back to campus, mindful of chores in the morning and the several pints of Guinness currently in my system. I had been envious but I also realised I didn't have to do this to myself. I was older now. I knew better.

13

Christmas and life became quieter. Students took their flights and their lifts away and I was left on my own. I took on extra chores to keep my college fees down–scrubbing out the kitchen, laundering in the laundrette, folding and putting away of quilts and so forth. An early talk I attended, The Meaning Of Cleaning, about cleaning from a spiritual perspective, was coming in handy.

    The storytellers were leaving campus for good as their course had been only three months long. A new bunch of blocked middle aged creatives would descend in the New Year. They didn't mean any harm but I was fed up of my peace being invaded with middle aged women hugging each other. I hate hugging. Storytellers were just so, well, emotional. Loving a community meal, they became upset if you declined an offer of their wholesome cooked food. It's not as if many of them were slim or anything.

    All the student houses were now empty. I regularly lay on the sofa with Lilly in the community room and began to read *Anna Karenina*–which I had borrowed unofficially from the library–and drank cava from one of the chipped champagne glasses I'd found at the dump. I was feeling that faded grandeur. I had had no idea Tolstoy had written so much about farming in pre-revolutionary Russia. I sympathised with the landless peasant.

    New year's eve–hogmanay–and I was listening to the radio with Lilly asleep on my belly whilst continuing with Tolstoy and a version of *Auld Lang Syne* came on the air. The recording from *It's A Wonderful Life* filled the room, the scene when George Bailey is reunited with his family and friends. I drifted off and remembered something from the previous year in the run up to Christmas. I had walked to the Christmas Fayre at Michael Hall school. It was one of those lovely winter days, cold and hard and quiet and it was one of the many days of my life that I had gotten used to–of being splendidly alone and comfortable with it. It had taken many years to arrive at this place but with sex drive diminishing through lack of use and the need for incompatible company at zero, I relished my time to walk, read, sit, idle, dream.

The school was built in the 1700s–it had high ceilings, Palladian architecture, light and airy. It was where the children of the rich grew up or, at least, the middle class and switched on.

I walked down the driveway and was met with the aroma of Tablehurst burgers on the barbecue. There was a farmers' market of sorts and lots of children around. Everyone was frozen to the bone but a happy air prevailed.

I stepped inside. The hall was brightly lit and stalls with Christmassy things were everywhere. There was a warm hum of chat filling the room. Lots of little fairy lights were draped around stalls selling handmade hats, jewellery, chocolates, moisturisers, toys, books, a million gifts. I never bought anything at these affairs. I had long ago mastered the art of appreciation without buying. Having stuff never satisfied for long.

I wandered down a flight of stairs in search of second hand books and found myself in front of a notice: 'Clairvoyant Medium Readings'. The door was slightly ajar so I knocked, intrigued. A fragile woman with grey hair opened it. "Hello," I said. "Are you the medium?"

"Yes", she replied. Her voice was high and sweet.

"How much is a reading?" I asked.

"Ten pounds for half an hour," she said.

"That sounds a good price! When are you free?" I asked.

"Right now," she replied.

I sat in front of her at a wooden desk. She explained she had had The Gift since childhood. And so it began. I was fascinated.

"Margaret, I'm getting the name Margaret. Does this mean anything to you?"

"Yes," I said. "It was my mother's name. In fact, it's also my first name although I never use it." I was hooked. There was no way and nothing about me which said what my unused first name was. I hadn't told her anything.

"Your life has been quite dire in the past," she said, "but you don't need that anymore." Her eyes were raised to the top of her head and she blinked repeatedly, tilting her head up somewhat. "What you're doing now is intelligent," she said. "You're being guided."

She was communicating with someone from my grandmother's generation–she could tell from the style of her dress–but I didn't recognise my grandmother from her description. My own mother wasn't mentioned again after the bullseye of the name at the beginning.

"You're going to find yourself travelling. There's a man. You won't understand and you'll disagree at the time. But later you will understand. This is your path. This man will play a part in your future. There will be a sign and then you will know."

"Know what?" I asked.

"You'll know you are on the right path. Can I tell you something more? You've got to get in the driver seat of your life. You're drifting. I need to tell you–there's changes coming and what you are doing is wise but you need to make more changes."

"I don't understand." Well, I didn't.

"It'll all become clear. There'll be a sign and then you will understand."

I was unsettled. She had it so accurate over my mother's name, I couldn't not pay attention. She looked liked my granny. She was speaking to my granny. I left intrigued and not a little confused.

My cava addled mind poured over this again whilst Lilly purred on my lap. *Auld Lang Syne* seemed to be on a radio loop this evening. It took George Bailey's Guardian Angel to show him the difference he had made, that he had been the richest man in Bedford Falls and didn't know it. He was rich in friends. I was lonely–true–but in the aristocracy of Spirit, I was Empress, a self-created woman–however flawed–a twilight beauty. I went back to *Anna Karenina*. Wasn't she the one who threw herself under a train?

14

I ran into Leo in the new term out in the snowy campus grounds and I stalled, seeing his leg in a calliper. Happy new year, *ça va*? How are you?"

"I'm good, the operation went well but I have to wear this thing for another month," he said. "It's a bit tricky in the snow."

"How's your Canadian woman? Is she married yet?" I don't know what provoked me, it just spilled out.

"She's *engagée*," he said. He used the French word. I was taken aback.

"You mean she's engaged?"

"No, she's in a relationship." If *engagée* was French for being in a relationship, I was definitely *vacant*. He looked dismayed.

"Will you still go to Canada?" I asked. I wondered how he would square that one up. In fact, I wondered how I would square that one up, with my law of attraction intentions going on. Was this the law working?

"Yeah, I'm going anyway," he said. It would seem not.
"Is that wise?"
"I bought my ticket so I go."
"That's a definite 'I'm going,'" I replied. Again, my path still blocked.

"Things change. Maybe they'll break up?" he shrugged. "But I've paid and I want this trip. She's selling me her old car so

I'm gonna work on a farm for a month and visit some winemakers around Toronto, drive south by the Niagara Falls into the US and meet up with the wine trade in New York city. That's the plan. Then I'm gonna drive across and find some winemakers in California, up through Oregon– there's plenty of vineyards there too–and back up to Canada. That's three months I can have on a tourist visa in the States."

"Wow, you've got it all planned. It sounds amazing," I said.

"Yeah, well ... I'm looking forward to it now. I've never been to the New World and I love planning a journey. Sometimes I think it's what I enjoy the most."

"It makes my plans for France and Delphine's seem so ordinary. France doesn't have the allure of the open road, not that I can even drive. Ooo–I'd love to go to America one day. I've always wanted to visit New Mexico," I said. There was no way I was going to ask to join him, although I wanted to. It would have to come from him. Besides, he seemed to be hanging onto his own romantic hopes.

"I went to see a therapist in France."

"Jesus. Really?"

"I used to see him a lot after I had the affair."

"Jesus. With who?"

"I got real messed up a few years back with a married woman but I got sorted out and that's when I went travelling, when I was better."

"Did he sort you out this time?"

"Yeah, so now I go travelling again. There's more to life than travelling and wine, I know, but not much more," he said.

"Books and music sweetie, books and music."

"Travelling, wine, books and music. I like it."

"Stuff work."

"I like working. I'm gonna write a blog for my trip, a diary, it'll be research for me."

"Good for you," I sighed as I walked away. It was time for class. Gosh, I envied him! I had to clear my thoughts and let go of negativity and opinions about how this summer of love could come about. It's on its way! Surely?

He was twenty-nine for heaven's sake and I was forty-six, a young forty-six and an increasingly slim one. I reminded myself I was removing my resistance to Leo being my lover and I was beginning to act in a way that might expect it. I counted my alcohol units too, Bridget Jones style and still, every day I wrote:

"I am so happy and grateful now that Leo and I are spending our summer together and are in love."

Bridget might have had her diary but Laura had her gratitude journal. Writing out gratitude lines every morning with coffee gave me a purpose. It cut into my psyche for the day and the physical act of moving my hand across the page released anxiety and made me feel I was achieving something. I began to daydream what it might feel like if it actually happened.

15

Oh! How I waited! It was a pain in my body. The gym, the walks, the trying to write, the fantasies, the gratitude journal were all a device to avoid the pain of waiting. I knew if I went directly for Leo, he would move away. I could sense it. My demeanour gave no indication I was waiting. My demeanour–and I was paddling hard beneath the surface–was nonchalant. I was happy and approachable and cool. Yeah. What if I waited and nothing came of it? What would I have learned? Would I rush at the next person I liked? Or would I go through another painful waiting? How long do you have to wait in life for life to come and get you? Love was proving as elusive as the Higg's boson, writing a novel even more of a mystery.

Somewhere, out there in the further reaches of my mind my novel existed intact. I had to align with it but a whole bunch of resistance lay on the path–impatience, mainly. They say the sign of maturity is the ability to defer gratification but I had an accelerator complex, I wanted everything NOW. If I could outcast myself further, further and further to reach my goal along an inner particle collider, all sides of my mind, left and right, conscious and unconscious, my ego self and my Higher Self could all come together as one, a supersymmetry with Universal Mind and I'd find my novel there. I consoled myself that the Universe was still expanding and time was on my side. The God Particle hadn't left the building, yet.

That night, I awoke in the time between worlds and I wondered why, as I often did in the middle of the night. Why? And then I heard it. It was the tap. Drip. Drip. Drip. Drip. I was in torture.

16

As I was intent on winning the affection of the French, I selected *Madame Bovary* to read next. She married a boring guy. What was it with these women? Bovary took an overdose, Anna Karenina under a train. I was beginning to wonder if all literary heroines come to a sticky end? At least Jean Brodie remained independent, even if she was deluded. She was Scottish. I resolved to write my own ending. I resolved to make any heroine of mine succeed. If I was choosing fantasy over reality, I needed to ensure fantasy wasn't a freight train that was going to run me over.

17

January 25th and Burns Night was approaching. The birthday of Robert Burns and I was the only Scot for a mile around so I took matters into my own hands and bought haggis. Leo would love a good haggis because most foreigners did, except the English, most of whom I knew seemed to worry about their health. It's not what you would call nouvelle cuisine, more a festival of cholesterol served with mashed potatoes and turnip, all the better to absorb the whisky and lull you into a coma for listening to poetry. Of all the people I'd cooked it for over the years, only the Hungarians declared it not quite lardy enough. Delphine and I had bought a bottle of Dalwhinnie together and a couple of bottles of beaujolais. I was beginning to wonder if maybe tonight would be the night, you know, when the Universe might toss a few coins in my direction. It was Burns Night after all. A night for poetry and lurve.

There were around twenty of us, Andrea and Suzanne included. The common room was candle-lit, the fire was ablaze and Lilly was standing right in front of it, her eyes closing sleepily and once in awhile she would fall slightly as she fell asleep and then stand up again. I borrowed some Burns' poetry and a bagpipes CD from the library which had been playing for hours. I'd been boiling up haggis, neeps and tatties since late afternoon and by 7pm we were ready. Delphine was dressed to kill in McDonald red tartan she'd found at the dump and walked into the room with the haggis on a silver platter. She read the *Ode To The Haggis* in a French accent. It was barely intelligible with a Scottish accent anyhow–but sexy or what?–whilst I took a ceremonial knife from the kitchen and cut into the beast. Dinner was served. I gave Leo a shot of the Dalwhinnie, together with a plate of haggis and hot, buttery tatties and neeps.

"I love this haggis. I can't believe I've never tried it before. It's real food," he said.

"I can't believe you like it with your palate," I said. "It's a kiss from the underworld." I added, poetically. "You'll understand tomorrow." It wasn't food for love I realised, it was too heavy. It was the food of friendship. Was it me or the Universe who was messing up?

Andrea and Suzanne were hogging him but worse, all the women in the room–Delphine excepted–fluttered round him like deconsecrated nuns. Their anxiety and need to please were palpable. I don't think Leo noticed, he just saw them as nice girls. I found him baffling. Did he really not know? I decided to read aloud Burns' *'Comin Thro' The Rye'*.

> Gin a body meet a body
> Comin thro' the rye,
> Gin a body kiss a body,
> Need a body cry?

I despaired. The Universe was not on my side this evening. I was suffering from terrible Burns. I would simply have to get Leo ALONE. Nothing could be achieved with all the oestrogen in the room. And it wasn't as if much of it was mine. I finished the haggis, drank more Dalwhinnie and gave up on the Universe that evening.

Alcohol units: stratospheric. Calories: beggars belief. Spiritual awakening? The next day I was in carbohydrate hell.

18

What did I know about the French anyhow?

Un, deux, trois ... they were good for wine, for food, for love. For troubadours, for garlic and snails, the guillotine. For Chanel, the revolution, for the *terroir* and the pissoir. The Eiffel Tower and the Statue of Liberty. The resistance and the *soixante-huitards*. For Cézanne, Renoir, Monet. For Marcel Duchamp and his urinal and for the auteur theory of French cinema. And for that troublesome old dog, who never seemed to lie down and die, René Descartes.

For Lourdes even, and Rennes le Château. The French also had not one, but two holy Marys at Les Saintes Maries de la Mer. There was Perrier and Vichy and sadly, Le Pen. That gold coast, the Côte d'Azur, and the Mistral, that fierce cold wind that helped drive the finest painter that ever lived to madness. Starry, starry night, yes France was the country that Vincent Van Gogh made his home.

I wished for the beauty of a Catherine Deneuve, a *belle de jour*, with the art and grace of a wealthy woman, not the one I was now. Pale, freckly, poor.

19

I'd stepped out of the shower with a towel around me and found a man in my room. It wasn't Leo sadly, it was a complete stranger. He said sorry and left. He was good-looking and I thought my luck could have been in but he marched right out again. I opened the door after him and said, "Can't you see there's a name on the door?"

"Sorry," he said again.

I saw him again at morning coffee break and we shook hands. He was from Barcelona.

"You've just banned bullfighting," I said. "Ernest Hemingway would be turning in his grave."

"The Catalans have lost their *cojones*," he laughed.

Another Friday evening and I had lurched home in the rain from my walk and it was so muggy I had to take my clothes off. First I turned the oven on in the attic kitchen and then I came to my room—there was Lilly at the door—and undressed. There was no point showering yet so I threw on some old clothes before placing a pizza in the oven. Ten minutes later still hot and dressed in a holey t-shirt and knickers I went to retrieve the pizza. I was reaching into the oven when the kitchen door opened.

There was the Catalan again. In other circumstances I could have been nice but I told him to clear off as this was a private flat. He said, "Can I have your number so I can apologise properly? I said, "No, go away."

Such was life at Emerson. Not enough men and always the wrong ones. So life tootled on with its minor infractions with irritating people acting out their early childhood traumas at your expense, wedging doors open, cooking for you when you hadn't asked and feeling rejected when you said no. There was an expectation to be nice here, as in good. It somehow shocked people to realise that it wasn't the case. Not with me, anyhow.

20

It had been a bad year.
     Some time later, I made it my quest to find a new calling. I trekked around southern Spain one winter and finding outdoor life suiting me, in a short space of time I found myself at Emerson. It wasn't a long pilgrimage but a short one.
     I hadn't achieved enlightenment in my forty-six years–I had given up pursuing it. I envied the guy who wrote *The Power Of Now*–at least his consciousness had broken through to the other side. Happy women were all alike. Every unhappy woman was unhappy in her own way and I was unhappy in mine.
     My trek around Spain wasn't a time of wandering after awakening, it was a time of simply wandering–still no awakening. A long quiet highway to nowhere. I had rearranged the cutlery on the table, that was all. I had become both powerful and fragile at the same time.
     They say an addict should never get too lonely, too hungry, too this and too that but I seemed unable to help myself and, over time, I either went out on my own or stayed in until I arrived at thriving on solitude and turned inward to books. I preferred non-fiction mostly, travel stuff until it dawned on me that all the spiritual writers I liked lived in Taos, New Mexico. I bought a Lonely Planet guide to the Southwest and fantasised about it.
     I had this idea that my life had to be perfect to write–of course, the opposite was the case. Life isn't perfect neither is writing. Writing comes from life. Writing comes from things

turning out different than expected. Things going wrong. My old poet friend who complained of my crossword style was a genius and an arsehole.

Time alone was good for staring at the ceiling. Time alone was good for trying to write. Sleeping on your own was fine too but being single year after year was a hell on earth, especially when someone gorgeous showed up and all your issues came to knock on the door to say 'hello' once more before disappearing again.

Lilly and walking kept me sane. The thought of Leo's body and soul drove me on. The thought of a normal life again where I could relate to the world with an in-built defence mechanism–a man. I pondered whether I had made an unalterable mess of my life. I had reached a peak of negative capability. I had passed through the twin tunnels of depression and loneliness and was emerging. I am emerging, I thought. Emerging is a noun for me now. I may never reach the other side.

It had been a bad year. As a bonus, my cracked psyche remained forever open and the other worlds advised me. I made my deal with the Universe. If the sun comes up in the morning, Universe, then so shall I.

I had raised the bar.

21

A trip to an agricultural machinery event in Lincolnshire was coming up—our tutor loved farm machinery in the same way I might love wine—and I put my name forward for it. I realised Leo was going too and when I bumped into him, I asked if he was going and said, "Can I sit next to you on the bus?" like someone on the opposite end of the fertility spectrum.

"Yes," he said. I was startled.

"You'll sit with me on the bus?" I felt stupid. I think he was starting to get the message. I promised I would bring chocolate and other goodies for the trip.

The day arrived in February, a group of students gathered at 6 am waiting in the dark for the hired bus. When it turned up, we could see it was yellow and ran on vegetable oil. I sat near the back at a window seat and waited whilst the other seats filled up and I gave off my best 'don't sit next to me' vibe. He walked through the bus, I relaxed my pose and he sat down next to me. "I've got the chocolate," I whispered.

I had hours now to get to know him under everyone's eyes. The trundle of the bus meant they wouldn't hear a thing.

We drank orange juice and later ate some chocolate as morning broke and outside the dirty bus windows, there was hardly a sign of life. Spring had yet to get started, it was truly the bleak English midwinter. The little sun emerging was acid sharp on the eyes.

Leo told me about his time working at The Dorchester in Mayfair. He had served wine to Tina Turner, Mick Jagger and Bill Clinton. He had tasted an 1811 *Château Yquem* but hadn't swallowed. I told him I'd had not so much a drink problem, but a life problem being stuck in London. Certainly, I was a lot happier and healthier now. Especially since I was sitting next to him.

The agriculture machinery was a bore. Who knew? A huge sign hung at the entrance, a blow up from a cover of Farmers' Weekly, trashing organic production. None of us were attracted to this style of agriculture—mostly we were into permaculture and growing our own food and keeping things as small as possible. There was little love of hard physical work from any of us in the class, working morning until night and the desire to control with big tractors and a profit and loss approach amongst us was non existent.

I made a conscious choice to walk around the exhibits with the others as I didn't want to look like I had hogged Leo for the day. I wanted to put the women off the scent and it worked. We reconvened on the bus journey home and again I sat with Leo or, rather, he sat with me and as the bus began moving I sighed and said to him, "How did you find it?"

"I can't stand all that machinery, it's not farming for love, it's farming for money. It's an industrial binge," he said. "We need a revolution in agriculture."

"I think we already had one, that's the problem and it's still evolving."

"Evolving … *non*. They're not creating health, they're making money," and with that he put his head on his bag and closed his eyes.

That night, back in the attic, it was pizza and rioja as I watched some old Sex and the City reruns. Single women in the belly of the whale.

The following day was Saturday and I was up for a 7 am shift to prepare breakfast for a weekend course. During coffee break, I sat in the common room for a rest and The Guardian quick crossword. I was puzzling over 10 across: 'A conspiracy without this (6, 6, 6)' when a few students wandered in, including Leo.

"*Bonjour* Laura," he said with a great big French smile.

"I've got it!" I yelled throwing my arms in the air, grinning like Schrödinger's cat— this pussy was a-l-i-v-e—

"*Bonjour* Leo." I wrote the answer then looked up and our eyes met. I realised we had cemented our friendship. The answer?—'single bullet theory.'

22

A week later I overheard Andrea and Suzanne discussing Leo in the common room. They were so very concerned about his trip to Canada. I was fed up of failing to act so I went to my room and sent him a text and got to the point. "I'm *chaud*. Mlle Laura xXx."

"*Chaud* can mean lots of things …" he texted back.

"*Chaud* as in hot Pigalle porno XXX." That should do it, I thought.

"Maybe I could give you French lessons? But be careful you don't get your fingers burnt!" I texted again, not quite believing my luck.

"Lesson one Saturday night at the Chequers Inn 7pm *s'il te plaît?*"

"*D'accord*. Please come prepared."

"*Bonne nuit et dort bien. Rêve de moi!*"

"*Non! Rêve à moi—bonne nuit* Mlle Laura!"

I realised that Saturday was February 13th, the night before Valentine's Day. What would Sharon wear? I didn't want to go over the top, being a farming student, so I wore my best jeans and a black vest with a black chiffon top over it that tied at the front and a sparkly necklace. I had coloured my hair so it was even redder than usual and I was my target weight. I was as fabulous as Sharon Stone.

The Chequers wasn't an attractive pub–it had flocked wallpaper, creaky flooring, red swirl carpet but lots of seating where you could have a quiet conversation. It also had an open fire. It wasn't frequented by college students, more by locals and farmers.

I ordered a Sussex sparkler–a rosé it being nearly Valentine's Day. It was a Sedlescombe Organic Vineyard Rosé Brut 2006 in actual fact. I knew the Sussex sparklers were winning competitions over the French and I thought Leo would be impressed. Maybe I'd win him over for some *entente cordiale*. I took the opened bottle and two champagne glasses and found a seat in front of the open fire. 'Wine of England,' it said on the bottle. 'The initial explosion of mousse is followed up by the sweetness of stone fruits balanced with the good acidity of crab apples. The finish is long, and well structured.'

I was getting excited. I couldn't wait to try an explosion of mousse. I couldn't wait to see if we'd have a long finish that night. He arrived half an hour late but my Sussex sparkler was still sparkling. So was I.

"What have you got there?" he said.

"It's Valentine's Day tomorrow. I thought I'd treat you to an English rosé. I bet you've never had this one before," I said at first blush.

"No, I haven't." He looked around the pub. It was quiet. It was romantic. It might have been a bit over the top but I figured why not? Isn't it what Sharon would have done? It was six weeks to the end of term and I had to up the ante.

"Shall I pour?" he said

"Ooo yes! Poured by a professional! It'll taste even better! The mousse will dance on my palate."

He poured two glasses, the mousse indeed frothed to the top and he waited, professionally, then poured some more. We clinked them together and I said, "*Santé!*"

"Cheers Laura! This is great."

"What do you think of it? Tell me!" He swirled the glass and dipped his nose in, laughing at the same time. He sipped and gargled the wine in his mouth.

"What do you think of the mousse?" I asked. "I've never heard of a mousse on wine before tonight. I thought a moose was a Scottish mouse."

"It's a great mousse. I've never tried an English rosé before. You've chosen well," he said.

"The vineyard is a few miles away. They're converting to biodynamic as we speak. They'll be the first English biodynamic vineyard."

"I never knew," he said. "I really like to visit vineyards and meet the winemaker, especially if they're biodynamic. It's all good research. Let's go and visit."

"Cool! I'm up for it. I've never even been to a vineyard before!"

The mousse was going to my head. My head was spinning, just like everything else in the Universe. I could feel my cheeks flaming pink as the wine and the red flames of the fire warmed me even more. Leo was beginning to look relaxed and flushed too. I'd cracked it.

"There's something I need to tell you," he said. "I'm not looking for a relationship." My heart sank. Did I hear right?

"Then what did you have to meet me here for? You could have told me this anywhere. You could have just texted me. And you're half an hour late."

"I couldn't tell you that with a text," he replied.

"Why not? It's not as if we've started anything. You could have told me this on campus. And now you've just set things up to fail." I was cross. I was fed up having my time wasted.

After all the months of writing in my journal every morning, losing weight and sorting out my inner beliefs about men, including I may add, the belief that the hottest French guy I had ever seen would ever be attracted to me in a million years, what with the seventeen year age gap, I had finally gotten this guy down to a personal meeting.

"What do you mean I've set things up to fail?" he asked.

"You've just wrestled control of everything. I mean, why did you bother sending me any racy texts at all?" I said.

"What does racy mean?" he said. His English was good and included plenty of colloquialisms but obviously 'racy' wasn't one of them.

I gave up and drank a sip of wine. The mousse wasn't flat but I was.

We talked about other things. He had me firmly in the 'I'm looking for a relationship' camp and that was that. Game over.

I decided to enjoy his company regardless. It was this or back to campus for the mainly female Valentine's event, surely a fate worse than– but I couldn't think of a worse fate. I could smell his fragrance–masculine, the rough smell of his fisherman's sweater, *eau de l'homme chaud*–and our shoulders touched. If he was a wine, he would be earthy, well-rounded, deep, easy on the palate, an aroma of earth and rain and with a real long finish. And he'd got good legs.

I've heard it said if you only meet guys with commitment problems then it's highly likely you've got them yourself. I had had only one commitment though–to get the hell out of London and find a new life. I thought maybe the world would end as we ran out of oil. I would look out my window in south London and wonder what would happen if it all starts to kick off and there's no escape. I had intuitively nudged myself forward by releasing my beliefs it was possible to get out. The London riots came two years later. I had claimed my get out of jail free card.

The ground was frozen hard and the sky was black and starlit as we walked back later, both of us feeling slightly pissed. As we approached Tablehurst Farm, it got darker still walking through a tree-lined path so I put my arm through his. Suddenly, he turned and started kissing me. The rosé was working! "Hey! You said you didn't want anything!" I exclaimed.

"Maybe it's the wine," he replied.

It was an uncomfortable kiss, not quite gelling but I wasn't going to give up. We carried on, I knew I would sleep with him if I could. My ship was coming in. It was problematic but I was in a man desert and here was hot young French porno delivered right to my farm door.

We passed the Tablehurst pig pen. "Hey Leo, we could go over and fuck next to the pigs!" That rosé was working. He was shocked and laughed. We made our way towards the college and passed a group going out for a Valentine's drink. Good luck, I thought.

We slipped into Leo's house, then into his room. *Oh là là.*

"I've got some great wine in the fridge downstairs. It's the best in France. I'm gonna go and get it," he said, switching off the overhead light in favour of a lamp. He turned on a little netbook.

"Pick some music for us," he said as he went out the door. I found Ravi Shankar on sitar. "I'm in India!" I exclaimed as he returned with a bottle of white wine, two glasses and a dishcloth. My heart strings twanged sympathetically with the music. "Now you are in France," he said, kissing me on the mouth, "and now we are going to drink something special." He held each glass to the light and gave it a light dusting. He uncorked the bottle and poured a small amount in one glass and gave it to me. He poured himself another. "This is a *Coulée de Serrant* 1996, it's the best wine in France. A biodynamic, natural wine. There isn't better." He swirled the wine in the glass and I did the same. He put the glass to his nose and inhaled. "Brown bread, it's almost nutty," he said as he shook his head in disbelief and stared into the glass, "The balance in this wine is incredible." He took another sip. "Nicolas Joly is a genius," he said. "Do you like it?"

"I love it but I love most wine Leo. Is Joly the winemaker?"

"Yeah, he gave this to me when I went to volunteer on his farm for a few weeks. I thought I'd bring it for a special occasion but I kept seeing it every morning when I opened the fridge …" He looked at his watch and held up the glass. "Happy Valentine's Day." It was midnight.

"Happy Valentine's Day." We clinked our glasses and sipped once more then made our way to the bed. We had already taken off our shoes at the front door. We started kissing. Soon all he was wearing was his friendship bracelet and a little beaded necklace around his neck. I wore less. "Have you drunk wine with someone naked before?" I asked.

"Naked wine drunk naked with a beautiful naked woman is the perfect combination," he said. He reached over for the bottle and poured us two more glasses, then a little bit more on my belly button and licked it off. All my chakras were spinning and the room would too if we drank much more. I drank a glug then took the glass from him and placed them both on the side cabinet. The time for talk was over and we made crazy naked love to Ravi.

"How do you find sex with me?" I hushed.

"Erotic," he replied. "*Baisse-moi*," he whispered in my ear.

We had a conversation after, as is often the case. "Have you got any more news for next summer Leo?" I asked.

"My plans are still for Canada but not for long 'cos my knee won't take too much heavy work. I've got the car, I've got enough money and I've found a French guy in California, a biodynamic wine consultant. He says I can work with him for a month helping vineyards convert."

"Oh! That sounds so exciting! So you'll still drive across the States? It's not like you need lots of farm experience. I mean you were brought up on one. Oh! What a good idea!"

"You wanna come?"

"Are you serious?"

"I dunno. No. It's work I have to do. I always travel alone. I like my freedom," he said.

"I like my freedom too but it wears me out. Tell me all the places you've travelled," I asked.

"All over Europe, Ukraine, Russia, Georgia to India and Nepal. I spent a year there on the tea plantations, vineyards ..."

"They've got vineyards in India?"

"There's vineyards everywhere Laura."

"There's none in Scotland–yet."

"The English *terroir* is getting better than Champagne's now."

"It's Sussex *terroir* that's better than Champagne. Aren't you supposed to be specific? I love Sussex."

"Yeah, I like it too but back to my trip. My return journey I travelled through Turkey and the Balkans. I was really putting off getting back home. I stayed ages in Croatia. Did you ever see a film called *Sideways* about the two guys on a California wine trip? I saw it in Croatia."

"God, I love that film! I laughed out loud when the naked guy ran into the car window! So you saw it in Croatian?"

"No, it was in English with Croatian subtitles."

"I once saw the film *Dracula* in Transylvania, believe it or not. If there's one thing I love, I love going to the cinema. I saw *Sideways* one afternoon in London and I was the only one in there. I smuggled in some chocolate and I bought a coffee and I took my shoes off and put my feet up on the seat in front. I was so depressed when I came out to find myself in Peckham in the rain. I loved that film."

"Yeah, getting back to France … it was a big problem. Three years on the road and then … France. I couldn't handle it so I've come here. At least I'm still learning. I worry I'll never stay still. You can't be a winegrower if you want to travel. You have to tend your vines."

"Oh, one day, you'll want to stay with your vines, *chez toi*, and everyone round the world will come and visit you to drink your wine." I gave him a kiss. "I'll come and visit and drink your wine–you can trust me on that." He grinned. "I hope you're right but I don't think it's gonna happen soon."

I twiddled with his beaded necklace and pulled him to me. I didn't want to let go, starved as I had been for affection for ever. The sitar music finally came to an end as did our kissing. "I love your little necklace," I said.

"I got it in Nepal, same place as the bracelet." He got up to click the replay button and asked out of the blue, "What year were you born?"

"1963. After the Beatles first LP. My mum went into labour when she heard President Kennedy was shot."

"1963," he repeated. I found it odd at the time but I realise now he probably was translating the numbers into French and then he said, "1963! You're forty-six!!"

I said, "Yes, I told you before."

"You don't look forty-six," he said. "I mean, you don't dress forty-six." He looked confused, if not panicked and all I was wearing was a birthday suit.

There were group discussions around the college about my age, although I didn't know it at the time. People were amazed. I wondered what planet they were living on. Didn't they know how fabulous Sharon Stone was?

I left at around 2 am. I had chores in the morning and the single bed was no good for a decent sleep. He didn't want me overnight anyhow so I departed before he had the chance to impress upon me again he might want control of everything. I was glad to leave for sleep. I was glad for my tryst.

I saw him again two days later surrounded by his pool of admirers.

23

It was the birds I noticed first when I moved to the country. In the winter it was better because they were on vacation to the southern hemisphere and the mornings were late to start but in the summer there was always one blackbird that started before dawn, one really noisy one and then it would shut up and I could go back to sleep. Not for long though, as they all got going at first light, and then came the sound of running water outside my window. And so I lived with the birds and the sound of the running water. I noticed mornings getting earlier. Spring was on its way. The end of term was coming and I was a running out of time.

Leo arranged a trip to Sedlescombe vineyard. Four of us headed off one Saturday morning in the March sunshine. It was still cold. There was Leo, Delphine, myself, Andrea minus Suzanne and Camilla from Argentina. She had worked in a winery back home and had applied to be agricultural adviser on The Archers. "What's all this about the *terroir*, Leo?" I asked as he was driving.

"It's the taste of a place," he said. "Wine is a living thing. A living being. It's unique to the time and the place that it's made. It's the earth, it's the sun and the moon and even the winemaker and the animals on the vineyard are included in the *terroir*."

"And if you make a natural wine, a naked wine," he continued, "so you don't mess it up with chemicals in the winery then you have the absolutely best method for the expression of the *terroir*. Biodynamics is the best way for growing grapes that can express the *terroir*. And it'll taste even better on a fruit or flower day."

"Wow. I didn't know the taste of wine would improve just because the moon is in Sagittarius. I've never heard of such a thing."

"Yep. A biodynamic and natural wine is a wine with emotion, a spiritual being, made with the help of the angels. It's in touch with the cycles of the earth and the seasons. It is absolutely the taste of place in every possible sense of the word. And you should drink it on the right day, it'll taste even better. The wine will be more expressive."

"And it won't give you a hangover either!" I laughed.

"There's no sulphur. A good wine label should say just this–'Ingredients: grapes'–that's all." The car fell silent. We were in the hands of an expert.

"It's a revolution this natural wine, it's stirring up a lot of trouble. There's a lot of money to be made in the wine world, you know, but a natural wine is all about your emotional response, it's unique to you. A technical wine, an intellectual wine cannot evoke emotion in the same way. Wine should transport you the same way music can, the way poetry can. The wine needs to sing."

"That's a lot to ask of a glass of wine," I mused. "Isn't the whole idea just to avoid a hangover in the end?"

"Well, the French like to drink so, yeah, that's definitely part of the story."

"What day is it today?"

"It's a fruit day."

The vineyard itself was still bare from winter and had recently been pruned in preparation for this coming year's growth. Leo introduced himself to the winemaker who showed us around. It wasn't a full farm with a range of animals and crops, neither would it be. It was simply a vineyard so in order to become biodynamic, it would have to incorporate some of these qualities. The main biodynamic method was the use of some specially made preparations. It could seem secretive to outsiders but only because it was so, well, nuts.

We tasted in the winery and I tossed from foot to foot trying to stay warm in a manner not conducive to a tasting. A large barn housed the winery and the door was open for a little shop. I tasted this and I tasted that. I listened to Leo speak and entertain the winemaker. He was doing a terrific job.

A dreamboat. Dressed in his best, speaking intelligently with that warm French accent. In his element. I dreamed of him even as he spoke, even as he was right there in front of me. He represented everything I had ever longed for–beauty, sex, youth. Sex. Beauty. What did I want from love? Why didn't I find a stable man with a good job appealing? There was no answer to this question. My desires for unsuitable men seemed to call my life forward. Into interesting times, sure, but into disasters as well. Why? Was it an electra complex? Had all men abandoned all women in the modern world? It seemed like it's what they wanted. Replaced by the state? Something was wrong here, was it just me? I couldn't get to the bottom of it. I was supposed to have a career. I was supposed to have had one. I hadn't. Men didn't like career women anyhow but I've got news for you–they didn't like it if you didn't have one either.

Somewhere, somehow I had dropped the ball and was alone on midfield. The thought arrived as I sipped the gewurztraminer. It was a system problem! It was structural. Industrial civilisation was built on a death wish. The death of God. No, not the death of God, that I could handle. It was the death of everything that was natural and good and a worship of the machine. The discovery of fossil fuels had allowed the male a privilege of dictating the terms–there was only one way and then there was the highway. Take it or leave it. Join the white male system of control! So how come it was men, or a certain kind of man, who seemed to be leading my life forward? I barely read books written by women anymore. I was puzzled by this state of affairs. Could it be that I had internalised a whole bunch of male values without realising it? Or could it be that without children, and without a desire for them, I was, in fact, as free as bird to follow any whim I fancied? Would I ever compromise myself and settle and belong? People were always telling me what I should do but no-one ever said–why don't you become a better human being? Why don't you be kinder as a person? Suggestions were invariably about 'a job'–as if being a corporate drone made the world a better place.

And so often I was perplexed at this until I gave up the analysis. I looked at these so called happy marriages and the ugly people in them and think who could have sex with that? Was I immature like my sisters said? Maybe, but didn't Picasso also say– and he was way brighter and more talented than my sisters–we are all born children, the thing was to remain one? Apparently most people were happy with their lot. It was artists and politicians who caused all the trouble. I wasn't a politician so I must be an artist. A tortured one at that. I was an artist without portfolio. Never mind, at least I had an *atelier* to live in.

I bought a little 50cl bottle of rosé and we reassembled for the car later.

Leo had bought a red and a white wine and said, "I'm gonna put them in my cellar in France."

They talked about going out that night to The Foresters again and I thought to myself, yeah, maybe I will and Leo said maybe he would too so I went to my room up to the attic, Lilly at the door, meow my lovely, and lay down with her purring on my belly. I started to cry. I wanted Leo so badly and felt so alone and I wondered whether he might call to go to the pub.

I didn't eat that evening but I opened and drank the rosé, it being a fruit day. I turned on the internet radio and found Celine Dion murdering *All By Myself*. I remembered it from Bridget Jones the movie and shuddered. Why did they have to do this to music? It had been a great song. The French were right to ban it. If they hadn't already, it was about time they did. I went onto youtube and played the original Rachmaninov piano concerto and breathed again.

I lay back once more and I remembered Leo's beauty that day and my body twisted with longing. Was there a way to have a life without a man in it and not to have to experience this humiliation? Another thought came to me. I had committed a cardinal sin. I was born female, therefore inferior. Worse than that I now realised, I was guilty of committing another. I was failing to link myself to a male to redeem the original sin. This was what was troubling me. This I had internalised with such shame without realising. The white male system of control had succeeded in colonising me, it had colonised everyone else too. All happy women were alike, but I was peculiarly, excruciatingly, millennially unhappy in my own way. But I didn't want to think like a victim anymore. Couldn't I experience life without judgement? I remembered a line from *A Course In Miracles*: 'I could see peace instead of this.'

I understood then why I had come to biodynamics and farming–it was the ecology, stupid. I remained on my bed, still half wishing that Leo might call. The call never came.

24

I hedged around him those last weeks in that last term, deliberately keeping myself out of sight. I knew any sign of neediness from me meant imminent death. Not death, no that's not what I mean. I mean death to the dream–that I might have him, journey with him and avoid the void that could be my future. In the middle of my life I had come to a fork in the road. Before I could take it, before it would ever open up, I had to restrain myself which was never a strong point but I could make myself scarce. Now that was easily done. Easy. *Facile*, even. In the meantime, I decided to buy boots.

    I made a list of my requirements. Black, tick. Leather, tick. Ankle boots with hooks, tick. Steel toe cap, tick. Acid resistant soles, tick. Boots for walking, working, carrying me. Black boots were the only footwear I ever owned. They had become my weapon of choice as I never drove a car, and was grateful for the speed they gave me when I felt anxious walking alone at night.

    I needed black boots to get me from A to B and back again but I had the feeling this year, I might need them to return me from the brink.

    I took the Forest Way for the last time and wound up at the shop for work clothes. It was a man's shop. No high heels here, no elegant evening slippers, just sheer brute strength get out of my way I'm a man work shoes. Just the ticket. A pair of acid resistant soles with steel toe caps would get me through the summer.

    A happy post-purchase haze filled my being returning through the forest. There had been a light rain whilst I had been shopping and now the sun was out, I noticed the individuality of the plants, alert like little soldiers lining my path. I spotted a young rabbit–hello rabbit–then a fox wandered across my line of vision. I heard a blackbird sing–hello blackbird–and whilst I passed Brambletye Farm, I could hear the cockadoodle doos at once with a wood pigeon coo-cooing, a starling, a knocking on wood of the woodpecker. A red robin bounced a little in front of me before flying off. The forest bristled in glorious complexity. Hello foot soldiers, hello woodpecker, hello trees!

25

Leo was in the computer room the night before term ended. He was frantic, finishing an essay. I asked him when he would be free. "I reckon in one hour."

"I'll be back," I replied.

I had nothing to lose. I went looking for my ring. I still had my grandmother's wedding ring and I kept it in a little box. I wore it often but especially when I was insecure. Sometimes I wore it around my neck, other times on my right hand. I found it and put it on my right fourth finger.

I put on my winter coat, hat and scarf and took my torch and walked my usual route to the village. At the top of Tablehurst Farm, I looked up at the big night sky. It was huge. A shooting star caught my eye just then and I made a wish. Oh! I wish! I lowered my sights and walked towards Forest Row lit up like a Christmas tree. I met no-one. I went into Wine Discoveries, the new wine shop in the village, and I bought a wine that I had seen on the shelf but had never tried, a Picpoul de Pinet, a romantic little wine, a grape from the Roussillon in south-west France.

Back in the attic, I picked up two wine glasses then made my way to the computer room. Leo was still there.

"I bought us a wine for the last night," I said, "Look."

"A Picpoul de Pinet! Aha!" He laughed.

I unpackaged the wine glasses. "Here." I held out the glass to him.

"Give the bottle to me to open," he said as his hand took the wine and bottle opener.

He stood up and took the knife and cut off the seal. He closed the knife, and took out the corkscrew. He screwed. He used the lever to slip the cork out. He poured first a glass for me and then a glass for him. "*Merci* Laura and cheers!"

"*Santé!* To our health."

He lifted the glass to his nose after swirling the wine. "There's a lot of sulphur in here," he said. He took a sip. "Yeah a lot of sulphur." I took a sip too but I couldn't discern the sulphur from the wine. I enjoyed it anyhow.

"Would you say you had a preference for red or white wine?" I asked him.

"It depends on the food but I think I prefer red overall. It's more complex and there's more to learn from a red than a white. I like character, depth and beauty," he said.

"That's exactly what I look for in a man! I like intelligence too—is there such a thing as intelligent wine? Perhaps there's more to learn from a redhead than a blonde," I ventured. "I think I prefer sparkling wine overall. Champagne makes me so dizzy I can't think but I settle for cava mostly. Hey, did you ever drink the Hitching Post Highliner pinot noir? It's the one that Miles and Jack drink in *Sideways*."

"No, maybe I'll find it in America," he said. "I don't think it's a natural wine, though." He noticed the ring on my finger.

"Are you married?" he asked.

"No."

"How come you wear a ring on your finger?"

"It's my lucky charm. It's on my right hand not my left. It was my grandmother's wedding ring. Do you have a girlfriend?" I asked him.

"No, but I've got a hundred and fifty women friends on Facebook. So why do you wear it?"

"I'd be lost if I lost it," I shrugged. I twiddled the ring on my finger. He came back with me to my room that night but left later to sleep alone.

The following morning, I met a hungover Leo coming down the stairs from the morning assembly. "I gotta hangover," he said. "It's the sulphur."

"For once, I don't," I replied, referring to my hangover-free state. "I'm leaving for London in two hours." I had a hangover from Leo.

"You still wanna come on my trip with me?" he asked.

"Yes," I replied. It was the truth.

"OK. You're creative. You're adventurous. And I'd like some company so let's give it a go. I warn you, I might not be good to travel with. And I don't want any of that nonsense." He was referring to sex. It had been my fault. I kept my mouth shut.

"You could meet me in New York for the drive across to California. I reckon it'll take four weeks."

"OK. Let's see how things work out." The Universe had, indeed, delivered. On the very last day of term, in the very last hour before I left the campus, Leo had invited me on the road.

He kissed me on both cheeks, French-style, and I left happy. I had choices. I was also rid of him now for good if I wanted. After some goodbyes, I returned Lilly with sadness to her rightful owner and left the college. Before I might head west, I was headed south. The open road beckoned for France and Delphine's family's farm. High on a probability wave, I first needed to drop some stuff off at my sister's place in Brighton. I didn't own much anymore but I had some papers and books and winter clothing that needed storage.

26

Mary was horrified to hear I might take a trip to the US. The fact that Leo was so much younger didn't help matters. She saw his photo on Facebook and said, "Why would someone like that be single? Shouldn't he be working on a Paris catwalk?" There was no escaping the traps of others. Maybe they were worse if you were exceptionally gifted in some way, like being a beauty. To be beautiful and single was against the rules. Even a man had to conform. I despaired.

We had met up for lunch at the Infinity Cafe on Gardner Street. Mary liked baked potatoes, or 'jackets' as she called them. It was her favourite food. In the multiplicity of cafes that Brighton enjoyed per person, per square kilometre, Mary had a not uncanny knack to home in on all the places that served 'jackets'. A nice little safe jacket potato. I opted for Infinity's all day breakfast of bacon, eggs, sausage, mushrooms, double bubble and a nice mug of tea, plenty of milk, two sugars. The food arrived with a sprig of basil–that was Brighton for you. As I poured ketchup on to the bubble and squeak, she said, "I thought you were going to settle in France."

"I thought I was going to settle in Brighton," I replied, "but I haven't made my mind up."

She unleashed a torrent. Shouldn't you be establishing yourself here? When are you going to settle down? You can't live like this forever. When are you going to get a job? And the prizewinner of all prizewinners that if I hadn't heard it myself, I wouldn't have believed that a comfortably married person would rain down on someone who was alone in life–

"Who's going to look after you when you're sick?"

Enough! I fled the wicked witch of the west and her fermenting cauldron and continued with my plans. I never got sick and I wasn't afraid of dying, never mind dying alone. I was to pass through the *Limousin* to make a visit to the wicked witch of the east–my eldest sister. Veronica was a *matterhead, par excellence.*

27

The *Limousin* is *France profonde*, lush and green, unspoilt cattle country. *Le Dorat* is a pretty enough place but dead beat in the winter.

Their B 'n' B was a 17th century townhouse with a large dining room. I hadn't realised it, but my brother-in-law was an amateur spiritualist and so, one evening, we took out a glass, placed it upside down on a dining room table with our fingers on and endeavoured to contact the previous owner, Monsieur Bonhomme. Sure enough the glass started whizzing across the table shuttering around in nonsense to the alphabet of letters and numbers we had written out in a circle.

I helped in the garden, yanking out weeds and the overgrown creeper on the wall. I dug a new planting bed in the stony garden and birds began to return.

Valerie asked as she often did–and she was mean about it too–when I was going to get a job or settle down. She slapped her hand on the garden table one day in indignation. Why did I never meet any men? My sisters' manipulations were thick, if not fast. I felt like a democrat in a family of republicans, tea party republicans at that.

I was a disruptive influence, symbolising everything that was wrong in the world. A woman! Alone! Adventure! Freedom! You think you're special but you're not! Why should you get away with it! How dare you say just because you're forty you can do what you like! I've got work to do! We're running a business here! Don't any of these places you visit have a job for you?!

Job? *Job?* JOB?! *NON!* Capitalism had destroyed the individual whilst pretending to exalt it but I kept that opinion to myself. I knew what she wanted from me–complete blind obedience. No! I'm running from a job and as it turned out so was the SNCF. I couldn't leave quick enough but the French train service were on strike. Fortunately there was plenty of *vin ordinaire* on tap to soothe me.

"Look at the mess of this place! The builder is ripping us OFF! I've been cleaning toilets all day!"

Living the dream was a peculiar aspiration. Along with being 'the best you can be', it carried a danger that mostly the ultra rich had to face–what the hell do you do when you've arrived and it isn't enough? A need to escape the UK and its dreadful weather and toxic politicians meant the poison was exported. I'm sure the French were depressed with their own politicians, they consumed enough Prozac after all.

"I've got the offer of this trip" I said. "Do you think I should go?"

"At least you'd be doing SOMETHING," yelled Veronica.

I showed the teenagers Leo's photos on Facebook. They were definitely in favour: I should go to America for a road trip. At least the girls in the family had the sense they were born with.

The SNCF were back at work a few days later and I travelled south. Delphine met me at Cahors station. The landscape had changed. From green and lush to the dry and dusty red of the southwest with its backyard swimming pools. Delphine took me to the market on the main square where her parents were selling their produce. We sat in a pavement cafe until the end of business. "What would you like to drink, Laura?" she asked.

"I'll have what you're having," I replied. And so it was that I tasted my first drink of sparkling water with mint syrup. She had ordered us both a *Perrier de Menthe*–it was like drinking toothpaste.

"How goes it Laura?"

"My sister has become a monster. France has created a monster. She was never like that back in Scotland. Then again, maybe she was …" I drifted off.

"She's jealous of you," said Delphine. "You have a lot of freedom."

"Is that it? Really? But I have nothing, I own nothing. I'm alone in the world," I said.

"For now, you have us here in France and you are welcome to stay and work all summer and we will look after you splendidly," said Delphine.

"I love Cahors. How come I've never heard about it before? It's beautiful. So much of France is lovely and it's emptied out in the countryside. The UK is so built up."

"I'm very happy to be home," said Delphine, "but I can't stay forever. I have to get a proper job by the end of the year or I'll go mad in the country. Have you decided on your road trip yet?"

"I haven't booked a ticket if that's what you mean. He was a bit of a pain in the arse," I reminded her.

"I remember but what else are you going to do?" she said. "It's an opportunity that all the women at the college would have died for."

"I know. It's just that even I think I should be settling down now."

"Rubbish. Settle down afterwards. Go. If it doesn't work–you come back. You'll never have the offer again. Let's face it, you can't even drive. Go! *Allez!* Isn't it what you asked for with the law of attraction?"

"Yep, it's what I asked for."

A white statue of the Virgin graced the entrance to *Château Bellelavie*, giving the place a numinous air. Delphine's parents were welcoming and embraced me as part of the family. They were happy, of course, for the extra worker and I learnt to properly milk cows from their herd of fifteen Brown Swiss which Delphine's brother Stefan managed. He would inherit the farm in time and just like in the old days, the farmer wanted a wife. Looking for the one was a perennial problem. We drank their stupendous *Clos de Bellelavie* with dinner, a black wine made from the malbec grape.

"Delphine, you know, we haven't had a conversation about anything other than a man for a while. Let's talk about something else–you choose."

"OK. Let's talk about farming," she replied.

"God, no."

"OK. Let's talk about food."

"That's the same as farming, but OK," I relented. "What's your favourite food?"

"Meat. I love meat. I can't stand these vegetarians." Spoken like a true Frenchwoman. We were eating *Boeuf Bellelavie* as I called it, beef cooked in *Bellelavie* red wine, slow stewed all afternoon.

"I was brought up on potatoes, you know." I started to laugh. "I read a book in the library at Emerson and d'you know what it said?" I was having trouble continuing to speak I was laughing so much, throwing my head back. "It said if you were brought up on potatoes, then you would have poor appetite control as an adult." Delphine, me and *maman*, *papa* and Stefan howled and roared. *Maman* began to slap the table, she couldn't control herself. "That's the whole of Ireland and Scotland with no appetite control. I mean, I used to have potatoes for breakfast!"

"Laura, I read that book too and it said coffee was for journalists! That's you–you're a writer and you love coffee! That's you!" Oh God, coffee and potatoes had done me in.

Two months later and I was still at *Château Bellelavie* and loving it. I'd been tending the vines, I was freckled, fit and healthy with all that good food, wine and company and my *franglais* was improving. Delphine and I had gone out to drink in a few Cahors bars. I continued to prefer Bar *Ouf* on the main square, mainly because the name made me laugh–*ouf* was a reversal of the word *fou*–mad.

One night in the *Ouf* over a natural Cahors malbec, a *Clos Siguier*–and eating cassoulet–I asked Delphine something that had been troubling me. "You know, Delphine, I read somewhere that when you meditate, when you evolve spiritually, that you will meet the being of your unredeemed karma before you can evolve further. Do you know what that means?"

"It means that before you can evolve, you have to complete your tasks in life, that's what it means," said Delphine.

"I don't get this stuff about spiritual beings. I don't think they exist."

"OK, well think of it as a part of your mind, your Higher Self, isn't that what you call it you new agers? Your Higher Self knows your path and if you don't fulfil your path, you'll die."

"I'll die?" I took a panicked sip of wine, it was fruity, but smoky as tobacco. "Jesus, Delphine, that's serious. You mean I'll die if I don't write a book? No wonder being an artist is hell," I said. "It's fulfil your destiny or die, unredeemed? And people think it's easy, like it's a gift." I was brooding into a tannic gloom.

"It is a gift and you'll suffer if you don't use it. Don't worry about dying Laura, maybe it just means you'll not progress until you get down to work."

"I'm fucked. No wonder I'm miserable a lot of the time."

"You're not miserable, you're fun, you just think you're miserable, that's all." Delphine laughed. "You could just lighten up, take it casually. Maybe it can't be forced."

"And what's your life's work, d'you think? What do you have to do to progress?"

"I don't think my journey is such a tough one, to be honest. I have a good family and we own land." She gave a gallic shrug. "I think I'd like to help people and one day, I'll get back to the land too. I love this wine we produce here. I've done the career, city living thing." She held her glass to mine and we clinked and took a sip. "This winemaker is showing at the malbec festival at the weekend. I'm glad you're here to enjoy it."

I had wine coming out of my ears that weekend, my lips and teeth were stained black for days afterwards, even my skin took on a purple hue but it was a lot of fun. The Valentre Bridge over the River Lot was lit up at night and the length of it was turned into a canopied tasting room.

Leo and I continued emailing back and forth. He was in Canada now, had bought the car from his friend and was working on a farm and exploring Canadian ice wine, or so I read on his blog. He had used the name I'd suggested–*Intimate Terroir*–and hadn't bothered to let me know. I was happy he had the name. I was annoyed he hadn't told me he would use it. I hadn't bought a ticket to go anywhere but I was seriously considering packing it all in and returning to the UK. It seemed such a leap of faith to meet him in New York but he was keen. What if he didn't make it across the border? What if he didn't show up?

One day, I was idly looking for flights online and one appeared–a cheap flight to JFK from Barcelona. Barcelona! I was as near Barcelona as anywhere else. I saw that flight and I knew it was mine. I had to think.

It was a one-off opportunity. I had the money, the time and the freedom. I was about to go and settle again and I don't like settling but I was feeling bad from not having a permanent home. I'd gone through the equivalent of a divorce to escape. I didn't want to be stuck in survivor mode, a comfy mediocrity. I wasn't necessarily thriving either, that was clear. Oh! I needed a revolution! Nothing short of a revolution would change my life–the life I truly wanted was held behind a veil. And if a revolution was what I wanted and a revolution was what I needed then it was time to go on. My desire itself was revolutionary. I needed meaning and that was something worth fighting for. It was the only thing worth fighting for. I thought it had been freedom, for most it was love– love wasn't always freeing though, oftentimes a trap. Meaning didn't depend on anything except my own mind. I could give my mind the gift of freedom to create my own meaning. Now that was a liberation theology I could live with.

I wanted to be in permanent fulfilment mode, not for stuff or status but for mySelf, the inner Laura, the one with the direct line to the Godforce, the creating energy. Failure was a belief, one I didn't have to entertain. Sure, it was scary, but this is life, it's meant to be. I could trust in the All That Is. After all, we were in a deep, lifetime 1-1 relationship.

I wish I could say I had intended the quest, that I'd got divorced or sacked and wanted a nice middle-class challenge to find out who I was. The trouble was I hadn't had myself reflected back to me for so long, I was beginning to wonder if mirrors existed.

I remembered my gratitude journal. I had written this specifically every day for months–

"I am so happy and grateful now that Leo and I are travelling together this summer and are in love."

Could It Be Magic? I had asked for the affair, for a travel companion and the Universe was delivering it on a plate yet the influence of the world was bothering me, telling me to conform. My whole life was an uncertainty principle. I could still step away, like I did from London, a free woman. Society wasn't designed to set me free–I wouldn't get freedom or meaning for nothing. I'd have to fight for it. Sure I might end up living in a wine barrel like Diogenes but would that be so bad?

It's what you asked for. You have to go to see if this stuff works. But could I risk not getting what I wanted?

With the coming of Leo began the part of my life you could call the beginning and end of my life on the road. I thought Leo would be a great guy for the road because he was a rugged individualist, albeit with major mother issues. I'd often dreamed of America and New Mexico, especially Taos where the hippies lived and even bought a guide to the southwest but I never took off. In the end, I went on the road because like Everest, it was there and I didn't have a better idea.

Snagged between time and eternity, I was cursed–or blessed–with a visionary mindset and had no other choice but to follow the call. The trip was an open door, if not into the future, then into mySelf. I had charged myself with the task of self-realisation, now was not the time to lose nerve. Like The Fool of the tarot, I flew in the face of reason and booked a transcendent flight into *terroir* incognita. I had died to my former self–in a bardo state–a new self waiting to be born.

There was a volcanic cloud hanging over Europe that day, one month to the day of the Deepwater Horizon oil spill in the Gulf of Mexico. Would consuming two transatlantic flights and a 3,000 mile car trip's worth of petroleum make much difference?

28

So I gave the Matrix the slip once more and in the summer of 2010, I set out to discover America.

First, a train south to Perpignan. I was in Catalonia now and there was a sense of Spain in the air yet I was still in France. Another train further south alongside the Mediterranean, the Pyrenees in sight. We passed through Collioure and Banyuls-sur-Mer with their ancient vineyards sloping down towards the towns, almost into the sea in places from high up in the Pyrenees foothills. I changed onto a Spanish train at Cerbere, travelling south once more through Spanish Catalonia this time, until I reached Barcelona.

I was at airport luggage check-in the following day before I realised I didn't have a label for my bag. I wouldn't be seeing my stuff again until America. Or would I see it at all? With no home address and no real forwarding address, did the Universe in its Universal Wisdom want my stuff back? If part of the pleasure of travelling was in the planning, why hadn't I done any? I hadn't even taken out travel insurance. I was on an extraordinary rendition. I flew to Dublin where I caught a connection to JFK.

I had made one plan, however. I'd made sandwiches. The night before on a stroll down the Ramblas, I'd bought bread and *Manchego*. It had been a sheltered life thus far, I realised, when the in-flight food arrived. Don Quixote himself had gone mad on a diet of books and I was beginning to think I needed to watch my step.

Leo had reminded me via email–don't tell them you're visiting farms when you're at customs. So I didn't. I was on holiday. For three months maybe. Did I have enough money for such a long stay? Yes, I replied. I didn't tell them I'd be sleeping in a tent. The tent that had survived two flights and no label to arrive with me.

I exited the airport building into the burnt orange evening then took a yellow cab with a driver from Uzbekistan. I told him I was taking a road trip. He said, "The suffering of the road is like the suffering of the grave." It was an Uzbek aphorism.

He delivered me to the Y on the Upper West Side, Amsterdam Avenue, at 9 pm Thursday 3 June 2010.

29

Friday was a flower day. The sun was shining as I awoke and I sang *Could It Be Magic?* in the shower. I put on my emerald cotton blouse and applied a little make up. Sipping coffee and poring over a map of Manhattan, I felt as good as a woman twenty years younger. Later I walked down Broadway, red hair a-flaming, intense as the summer heat. I was out to win the heart of a man.

    The Clo wine bar, on the fourth floor of the Times Warner Building at Columbus Circle, was tiny. One room with a view–what a view!–no sign of Leo. I sat on a high stool at the long narrow table surrounded by walls of wine bottles in glass cases, the wine list projected along the table's length from an infrared lens on the ceiling. As I hovered my hand over the list, the projection changed showing one bottle at a time with tasting notes. It was a theremin of a wine list and I was in need of a drink. An Austrian Nikolaihof Riesling 2008 I'd read about on Leo's blog seemed a good choice. White, dry, natural, biodynamic. Everything I could possibly want in a wine glass. It was $10 and they asked for a credit card. "I don't have one," I said. "I'd like to pay cash."

    I imagined myself in a *Sex and The City* episode as I perched on the stool playing with the theremin, I mean, the wine menu, glass in hand. I heard the voiceover–'Clo was the latest happening wine bar in town. Leo was late. When he arrived, Laura was a little drunk. He was wearing beige.'

"*Bonjour* Laura. How are you?" His beauty was startling and I was hooked once more. He gave me the French kiss cheek thing.

"Hello. I'm good. That's some jacket you're wearing," I said. It had a million pockets.

"It's my travel waistcoat. I've got everything here. Passport, wallet, map, money, I'm robber-proof. I bought it in Nepal." He looked me up and down. "You're wearing green. It suits you. You should wear it more often," he said. "You gotta wine already, that's just like you."

"Well it's a flower day. It's a Nikolaihof." I swirled the wine in the glass. "A wine blogger recommended it –it's giving me good vibrations."

"I recommended it too."

"The wine blogger was you, silly. Are you going to have one?"

"No, I wanna talk to the manager. It's cool here isn't it?" He was looking around.

"What do you think of New York?" I asked.

"It's as far away from farming as you can get. I'm going to Brooklyn this afternoon."

I offered him my glass for a sip. "Hey, if you go to Brooklyn you could get pizza from that restaurant at the beginning of *Saturday Night Fever*."

"I've never seen *Saturday Night Fever*."

"Tony Manero struts down the street and orders pizza from a window. He eats two at a time. One slice on top of another. I can't believe you've never seen it."

"I'm not a film buff, I'm a wine guy." He took a sip from my glass. "What I love about this wine is the long finish." I had drunk a European wine lake over the years but for the first time I understood a long finish. Finally, I had drunk something of value.

Leo had his professional conversation with the staff. I liked these people. Intelligent, liberal, educated, informative and, what's more, interesting. Better than that, good-looking. I was a little intimidated so I kept my mouth shut. Perhaps wine professionals give a good impression because they are just that: professional. But then I remembered a million dullard professional types–*matterheads*, all. There was something about the world of wine. It was a cultural connecting tool to smooth over the fact that most of us were quite frankly on the piss.

Leo sat down next to me on a stool. "How come you're not buying a wine?" I said. "Isn't it the done thing?"

"I won't get through the day if I taste wine everywhere," he said. "Besides, I'm here to look at this electronic menu, not to taste the wines. They're mostly not organic anyhow." Saturday would be busy for him but he suggested meeting up again on Sunday morning and taking the ferry to the Empire State Building before we left the city. "Can you find a Route 66 map? I haven't got the time to go looking for one."

"OK, but why?"

"'Cos we're gonna drive it to California."

30

There was a Route 66 section in the Barnes and Noble on Broadway. No maps, plenty of coffee table books. We'd be travelling through New Mexico, I realised, and a shiver came over me but the road only passed through the southern part of the state not Taos where the hippies lived and to where I'd always been drawn. I bought the *Route 66 Traveler's' Guide and Roadside Companion* and continued up Broadway. Periodically, I clutched my pockets checking for passport and money. My boots were proving too hot for a heatwave so I bought a pair of open-toed sandals with rubber soles for $14 from a drugstore. A bargain. I gave Broadway my regards and went back to the hostel.

Next morning, my body clock all over the place, I was awake at 6 am and I wandered out onto Amsterdam Avenue. It was quiet. I gazed in wonder down the length of that big avenue. People often say that life isn't like it is in the movies, but I beg to differ: on this particular morning, it was.

As I crossed the road I came across a black man in a wheelchair and he asked me to help him mount the pavement. I took hold of the handles behind him and tilted the wheelchair lifting the front wheels onto the kerb. I pushed him and his chair a few yards to his apartment door. He smelled of alcohol.

"I've been up all night partying," he said.

"Was it a good one?" I asked.

"It was good enough."

"I can't believe your friends would leave you like this to get home alone."

"Where's that accent from?" He turned the wheelchair to face me at his door.

"Scotland. This is my first time in New York."

"I've lived here all my life," he said.

I found a store selling coffee, bought a cup and a *New York Post* and sat on the bench outside the hostel door. Everything I knew about New York came from *Sex and The City* and I was looking for the listings for *Sex And The City II*. There was a 9.30 screening at the cinema on 84th and Broadway, a short enough walk away according to the tourist map. I decided to go in a New York minute.

A jetlagged, heat-waved altered state had me in its grip as I walked up Broadway later, after the film. Being in New York and watching a film set in Abu Dhabi had me more than disoriented. I wasn't far from a panic attack. I needed food. Further uptown, I came to a diner, bought a *New York Times* from a kiosk and entered to sit in a corner booth. Coffee and a Virginia Ham Sandwich. That sounded American. Closing my eyes for a moment, I asked the Universe for a message. Whatever my eyes rested on once opened was to be the answer.

'Tom's became a legend,' said the menu, 'through Suzanne Vega's song *Tom's Diner* and even more so after appearing repeatedly on the world famous Seinfeld TV programme'.

My mind flipped. My consciousness was expanding all over the place. It was life, the multiverse, everything. I asked the Universe for a deeper meaning. 'Waves Of Oil,' said a newspaper headline at the next table. It was still the ecology, stupid. I looked over the menu again but today's specials didn't include a bowl of quantum soup.

Just then, the waiter came and poured me a refill. I had time on my hands and I wouldn't meet Leo again until tomorrow. What to do? I opened up the paper and found the crossword. The first clue: 'US woman painter'. Well the one I knew was 'O'Keeffe' so I filled it in. Just like that, I resolved to see a Georgia O'Keeffe that afternoon. There had to be one in New York somewhere. I asked the waiter. He said, "Try The Met. It's in the park."

I heard church bells ringing as I left the diner, taking the unfinished crossword with me. I walked back down Broadway and re-crossed Amsterdam then Columbus and entered the park. I stopped at a pond for a rest and watched the ducks.

Phoebe Caulfield floated into my mind, you know, Holden's sister? Didn't they go to the park zoo together in the novel? He wants to be a catcher in the rye, to save children falling off a cliff. She says he's got it wrong: the Robert Burns' poem doesn't mention a catcher in the rye–it's coming through the rye. Holden got it wrong about the ducks too. They're here all winter. She was a heroine that Phoebe, not a phony! She saved his life. She knew Burns' poem and was only ten years old. I was fed up with boys' coming of age stories, truth be told. They weren't universal, they just annoyed me.

Good old Phoebe. I wished I'd had a younger sister who could recite poetry. It would have been a delight to look after her and show her the way. Another thought bubbled up in that moment. Could it be? It could be the truth–my sisters hated me. Why was nothing I did ever good enough? I had nothing they could possibly envy. Was I the ultimate red flag? If their domesticity was so great, wouldn't they be happy and nicer to me? And wouldn't I have chosen it for myself? They wanted me to fail to make themselves feel better. I'd been under attack all my life but I was a real person, not a *matterhead*, an active agent in my own life, no custom-made life for me–I'd made it all myself. All my mistakes were mine and weren't they glorious? All mine.

No wonder I thought the world was out to get me. In my life–it was. It had to stop. I was at risk of becoming a one woman entry in the *Diagnostic and Statistical Manual of the American Psychiatric Association*. McLove Syndrome. Even insanity had to have its fashions. To be sane in this society? Madness. I wouldn't give my consent to the consensus reality. I would Refuse with a capital 'R'.

Later that afternoon, I arrived at the Met and found the Georgia O'Keeffe's. Good old Georgia. She took on the big boys with her magnificent flowers.

Wandering in the greenery later, I found myself on Literary Walk. I couldn't believe my eyes. There he was–Robert Burns, or rather a statue of him. I marvelled at it. Poetry, love, art, that was the meaning of life–not business and commerce. He was a farmer to boot. I loved Robert Burns. He was a womaniser but I forgave him. Had he been good in bed? Big drinking–the curse of all poets–would have interfered, but he was still a man *for a' that*.

Back at the hostel, I got on the wifi lying on my bed exhausted–there were twenty five signals around. This wasn't just a heatwave I was going through it was a microwave. My pineal gland was being calcified out of existence as I picked up an email from Leo asking to meet outside the Stock Exchange the following day at noon.

31

The following day on Wall Street, Leo asked, "Was the Stock Exchange ever on *Sex and The City?*"

"Actually, it was," I said. "Carrie arrived in a rush one morning and pressed the bell to begin the day's trading. The *New York Star* had just got a Dow Jones listing. She wrote her column for it."

We settled in the end for the Staten Island Ferry. It was free. Do you hear me New York? I asked. The Staten Island Ferry wailed. Then the noise of the boat engine and the chatter of tourists. A city doesn't speak the same way people do–not that it doesn't have a spirit, of course, it's just that you have to tune yourself in and stay awake for the nuanced answers. They may not arrive in words but in a feeling, a moment, a car number plate, a bubble of a picture in your mind but you can ask a question to the energy of anything, even if it's nuclear.

I kept an eye on Leo. He would disappear out of sight, taking photos–always taking photos. I had been keen on photography too for a time but I was forever missing the moment, not the moment of the photo but for the present I was living in. So I gave up photography in favour of the present, except it was such a difficult place to stay.

We reconvened that afternoon and took the underground to Penn Station with all our stuff. I trailed after him through the streets to the overground. He walked so fast.

"I hate it you walking in front of me like this. I can't believe men still do this shit, it's so unnecessary," I said. We got lost and slowed down to ask for directions and had to reverse on ourselves and I thought I might lose him. He stopped to look up and said, "We're on Fifth Avenue." I looked up too and saw the street sign and so we were. We took the overground at 33rd Street to New Jersey where he had parked the car.

How the hell would we cross America in this? A black Saturn with a Canadian number plate. Leo had named it Black Beauty but it was a rust bucket, an RB not an RV.

He opened the trunk. It was packed with boxes of rice, pasta, lentils, salt, herbs, olive oil, chickpeas, peanut butter, tomato ketchup, canned tuna. There was a box with four Riedel wine glasses. He had everything covered. He pulled out a giant water cooler bottle and a plastic tube and I added my tent and rucksack.

"Here, take this," he said, handing me an extra car key as he opened the driver door. He took off his travel waistcoat and hung it around the driver seat. All his cash was in the waistcoat. "I don't wanna bother with ATMs," he said as we settled ourselves in the car. He put the water bottle on the back floor with the tubing. He found some string for my key and I tied it around my neck. It dangled at my belly button. It was then that I noticed his trousers, beige with a drawstring waist.

"I like your trousers. Are they linen?"

"They're made from organic hemp fibre. I got them in Nepal."

"That's so cool."

"They're good for driving. These tyres will need replacing en route," he said, changing the subject, and we were to share the cost. It had cost him $500 Canadian dollars to buy the car in Toronto.

It was 3 pm. He hesitated for a moment then reached to open the glove compartment. "I have something for you. I found a few of them back in France and brought one all the way for you to have. Here." In his hand was a turquoise, red and green friendship bracelet.

"All the way from Nepal?"

"All the way from Nepal. All the way through the Balkans to France, flown to Canada and driven right to you here in

New Jersey." I held out my left wrist as he tied the knot of the bracelet for me.

"I love it," I said. "We're friends now."

"Yep. You are *mon amie*. Are you ready Mademoiselle Laura? This is it. *On y va?*"

"*On y va!*"

"Let's go!"

32

We drove under the Hudson at the Holland Tunnel and crossed Manhattan. I could see more of the city now than in the few days I'd felt hostage to the heat and panic. I still felt claustrophobic sitting in the car. I don't know how Leo managed to drive. A foreigner in a foreign land–it couldn't have been easy.

We crossed to Brooklyn on the Williamsburg Bridge and drove north with the Interstate 278. I peered out at the Manhattan skyline which was obscured by Leo at the wheel. "God, it's amazing, Leo. Look!" He turned and gave me his camera. New York from a distance. It was magnificent but I was small and lost and in a car with a man I barely knew wheeling along to God knows where and I messed up the photo.

We turned onto the Long Island Expressway. There wasn't much to see now–cars, tarmac and trees. In the glove compartment, there were a million maps and on the back seat, more maps borrowed from his Canadian friend and then some picked up at the Canada border. I started a budget for totting up shared costs of gas, coffees and snacks, road tolls. I asked Leo where we were going to sleep that night. He said, "We'll find somewhere."

We made a stop for gas and then he filled the water bottle and placed it on the floor behind the driver seat. He stuck the plastic tube in the neck and sat facing the front, holding the other end of the tube in his mouth and sucking. This was his watering system. "You want some?" he said as he finished.

"Sure." I took the tube and sucked water too. "You're a genius," I said and passed the thing back to him, "I think." He recovered the bottle with the lid and we drove on.

Approaching sunset, we took a turning south and found ourselves with ocean on either side of us. Blue sky, blue ocean, white sands, white surf onwards towards the Long Island Ocean Parkway. I was in a wonderment. We were quiet. Leo would take care of everything. We crossed back north on the causeway later, looking from right to left, unable to take it all in, beauty everywhere. Back onto the freeway, the I-495. "Are we heading west now?" I asked.

"No, we're heading east."

"But on the map we're heading west. Are you sure?"

"You see the sun back there? That's the west. We're heading east. The sun sets in the west, Laura."

Towards nine o'clock, we were driving through a town when Leo pulled the car over in a parking lot next to a baseball field. There were men playing in floodlight. I asked him why we had stopped.

"We gotta stop for the night. There's a field over there and I'm gonna park the car. We'll just have to wait a while until it gets darker."

"OK. I'm happy enough to sleep in the car."

"NO. The car is for me. You gonna have to put up your tent."

"Are you out of your mind? We're in town!"

"I'm not driving anymore. I'm tired and I wanna sleep. Maybe I'll get up early in the morning. I got laundry to do and calls to make and I'll be able to meet you later."

"You mean you'd get up and drive off without telling me? How would I get in touch with you? D'you think I'd hang around the tent all day in the middle of town? You're out of your mind! You know lunatic comes from the French for moon? You know, *lune*. You're insane. You'd have my passport and money and everything!"

"This is MY trip. I got work to do. It's not a holiday. I don't want you interfering. You knew that. I mean, why'd you come along? I don't want to have a relationship with you."

"You don't just go off and leave someone in a foreign country without telling them first. Especially when they might have left their passport and money with you." I started to cry. Something I hadn't done in months. "You asked me to come! It's what you wanted! We have a relationship whether you like it or not! That's because you invited me! We haven't started on this trip and you're laying into me. I'm tired too. I was so happy a minute ago and now this!"

We argued some more. Abruptly, he started the car and drove in the darkening light onto the adjacent field close by some trees. We were in suburbia. I pitched my tiny tent beside the car, hidden from the road in the dark.

I didn't sleep. I had taken my passport and money into the tent with me. The honeymoon was over. I was as far away as possible from being Sharon Stone.

The following morning, I got up at six, packed up the tent and sleeping bag, sat on my rucksack and waited. I had barely slept. I saw a yellow school bus pass on the road, the first I'd ever seen. People were getting up and starting their day–a normal day to them. I wondered if they realised they had a couple of wayfaring vagabonds in their midst.

33

Leo didn't stir till 7.45. When he walked off to have a pee in the bushes, I sat in the passenger seat of the RustBucket, one leg in and one leg out of the open door and stared into the middle distance. I drank some water from the godforsaken tube thing. I needed a bank to withdraw cash. Did I go back to New York? Straight back to the UK? It would have been better to have this bust up in New York City. I said nothing. Leo busied himself boiling water on a camping stove and sorting through his clothes.

Laura! What have you done? I heard a sound. It was the sound of my own misery. If romantic love was akin to the great mythologies, then tilting at romantic windmills was living my own. I could have my fairytale, but I might not have the fairytale ending.

"I got some hot water here if you want a drink," called Leo. "This is camping, this is how it's done."

"I've been camping. I know how it's done." I got out of the car and made myself a cup of sweet black tea. "I've done lots of travelling before," I said. "Usually travel companions look after each other." I stood and watched the yellow school bus pass by in the other direction. "I gotta do a laundry," said Leo.

"If you don't want me here, tell me now. I need to find a bank and get back to the city. You have to help me," I said.

"I'm not driving back to the city today. There's a winery visit tomorrow."

"OK. Then if this doesn't work out, you take me back to New York after the winery visits." We agreed on giving the week a try.

We packed up and drove a few kilometres to a small shopping precinct with a laundry and stayed there most of the day. A calm descended–mainly because we didn't spend time together. I spent the day drinking coffee, reading and exploring the shops whilst Leo washed his clothes and began blogging away in a Starbucks. By 6 pm I was bored so I decided to eat at the American Diner across the road. Leo had never heard of an American diner before and came too.

This diner was all an American diner should be, a total walk back to the fifties. I wasn't keen on the fifties as such. I hated the clothes, the music, the coupledom, the conformity, the bras. I was a child of the sixties but the sixties had eaten itself. The sixties, even the seventies was the generation for me but it was hats off to the fifties for the diners. I mean, let's face it, where's the style in a sixties vegetarian restaurant? Nowhere, that's where.

Leo picked a table as the early evening sun shone through the window, casting a sharp light on his face. He couldn't sit still, neither could he look at me properly. He was up and down like a yo-yo taking photographs. "I love the décor," he said.

"It's stylish, isn't it?" I said. I ordered two beers and two portions of fries. I felt as stressed as ever. It was impossible to talk to him. I was increasingly irritated by everything. "Hey I've got fries for you Frenchie. Come and sit down." As our food arrived, we began to talk. I gave him a tip to write faster for his blogging. Just write, don't edit. Get all your thoughts down then edit and add the facts later because they were two different processes, they used different parts of the mind. He responded negatively. I changed the subject to diners, Americana, life, until I mentioned when I'd been unhappy once and he began to freak out.

"I don't wanna hear about it. I'm not a psychiatrist. If you've got problems, you need professional help."

"I don't have problems. Not now. I was just having a conversation."

"I don't want to hear about it. If you need professional help, you gotta get it."

"I don't need professional help," I replied. It was a bit rich coming from a reformed junkie who couldn't sit still in front of me for twenty minutes. We finished our fries in silence. I wished I'd come alone.

We camped at Montauk Point that night, the state parking lot. It wasn't as bad as it sounds because it was isolated with just one car–ours. Leo parked at the far end of the lot and I pitched my tent on the grass next to the trees, obscured from the road.

My first night spent sleeping in a parking lot went well. It rained in the night but I was comfortable and warm. I was awake when I heard the car door open the following morning. I packed up the tent whilst Leo used his camping stove to boil up water for tea and washing. We had oatcakes and cheese for breakfast. I made a mental note to buy coffee and creamer. Afterwards, Leo cleaned his teeth with a stick.

"I like your camping stove. It's cute," I said.

"I got it in Nepal. I used it for over a year on my return trip from India," he replied. "It's good to be using it again."

We started for Bridgehampton. I turned on the car radio. It was The Doors, *Riders On The Storm*. "Do you like The Doors?" I asked.

"I don't know anything about them."

"You don't know who Jim Morrison is? There was a film made about The Doors a few years back."

"No. I'm not a film buff. I'm a wine guy. I don't do music. Not much anyhow."

"He was the lead singer. He's buried at *Pere Lachaise* in Paris."

"Who's *Pere Lachaise*?"

"It's not who, stupid. It's the name of the cemetery. It's a really famous place. Didn't you work in Paris?"

"Yeah, I worked at *La Tour d'Argent*. Three Michelin stars but all I had time for was work and wine."

"Don't you know who John Lennon is then?" I was testing him.

"Yeah sure, he was in The Beatles." He knew I was on to him.

"He was shot by a Frenchman at the Dakota building."

"Really? Where's the Dakota Building?"

"In New York. FYI–he wasn't shot by a Frenchman."

Bridgehampton and our second Starbucks. Coffee. Papers. Internet access. Just as I liked it. Leo at one side of the coffee bar, me at the other. Him blogging, me online with my own little netbook then it was time for a walk. I walked into Black Cat Books and found *Eat Pray Love* by Elizabeth Gilbert. A book about a spiritual journey suited my mood.

Leo and I shopped at a supermarket late morning for food supplies–coffee, creamer –and found ourselves at the stationery section. I bought an A4 hardback purple notebook with black cloth binding for $3. It made me happy.

We got back into the car and as we drove off I pulled the notebook onto my lap and in the white space on the cover of the notebook I wrote on the first line:

'America',

and on the second line

'2010'.

"So you gonna be a writer Laura?" he asked.

34

In pursuit of the slow, the artisanal, the locally sourced, the virtuous, the organically and biodynamically grown, free of additives, earth-friendly wines, we raced the Rust Bucket along the roads of Long Island.

Channing Daughters Winery planted its first vines in 1973. We toured the sculpture vineyard and poked our fingers in the soil, then tasted wines in the winery. They like to blend wines here. Sometimes the blending is in the vineyard, the different grape varieties grown together. Sometimes the blending is in the cellar. They believe in being sustainable although not exclusively organic because, as the winemaker explained at the tasting table, all wines end up with some sulphur and copper in them to ward off mildew and these minerals have to be mined from the ground.

Around thirty wines were laid out in a line. We twirled and sniffed the 2008 *Sculpture Garden*. I sipped. It was as locally-sourced as you could get on this maritime climate yet dark, fruity, earthy, coffee and smoke. I uttered not a word. I hadn't a clue about wine though I had drunk it all my adult life. I viewed a bottle of wine as one of my five a day. I liked sparkling wine best.

Leo was amazing again–knowledgeable, sociable, funny, intelligent, holding his own. I wanted to contribute.

"How come you got so into wine Leo?" I asked.

"It's in my blood. My parents are farmers and wine makers. Wine is a product of agriculture–people forget that. It's a normal part of French farming. It's an agricultural product."

"I suppose it is–I don't usually think of wine like that."

"One day when I inherit the farm I'll turn it back–no, forward–to natural farming, a full farm with a vineyard. Biodynamics is the best way to retain the *terroir*–the full complexity of the place. We are *terroiristes* us new wine makers–stuff convention and Robert Parker and his wine ratings! We are going forwards to natural farming and we will win because the beauty of wine is," he gave a gallic shrug, "the beauty of wine! It's unique. And when something's unique, you can charge what you like for it. People will pay."

"So it's about the money?"

"No. It's about the *terroir*. I am a *terroiriste*."

We moved on to a Sauvignon Blanc *Mudd Vineyard* 2008 made from grapes grown on the North Fork. Still a taste of Long Island but now a clean, crisp, dry white.

"It takes a poet to make a great wine," continued Leo. "I like to think of a good natural wine as a living being. But I think a natural biodynamic wine is more than that, it's a spiritual being and it's a spiritual experience to drink it."

"I'll drink to that." We all three swirled and sniffed. I saw the ocean in my mind's eye as I sipped. God the wine was good.

That evening, we returned to Montauk Point parking lot to sleep again. We chatted about this and that in the car, about America. I liked Long Island. I liked the domestic architecture, the wooden houses with porches and rocking chairs on.

"I'd like to live in a house like that," I said, pointing out the window. "I'd like to sit on a chair in the sunset with a glass of sparkling wine and think about the day."

"You could build one on my farm," said Leo.

"But it's not your farm."

"It will be one day."

"You wouldn't want me living there. You barely want me on this trip." Suddenly Leo told me I talked too much so I shut up. I liked Americans, it was the French I was having trouble with. When the silence had gone on, he then said I was too quiet. I turned on the radio. "Do you know what this song is?" I asked. He knew nothing about music.

"No. I don't know music. I told you that."

"It's The Eagles, *Take It Easy*."

"Maybe the Universe works through technology?" laughed Leo.

"The Universe works through everything, stupid."

The next day driving along Montauk Highway to Bridgehampton again, Leo uncovered a problem with the RB. "The indicator lights aren't working properly. I gotta go and find a garage," he said. He dropped me at Bridgehampton Starbucks alone and my heart sank. I didn't know the car number plate. What was I thinking of? They say the Hamptons is a place of wish fulfilment but I wasn't a wealthy person with the problems of the wealthy, I was a poor person with a poor person's problems. A low net worth individual, my self worth wasn't that high either. I had his cellphone number but he listened to his messages just once a day and I didn't have a phone. I was a hostage in the Hamptons. All I could do was wait.

"I am so pleased to see you," I said as he walked in the door at 3 o'clock. "I left a message on your phone. I had to borrow one from another customer. I was trying to figure out what I'd do if you didn't come back." He was incandescent with rage. "What happened?" I asked.

"I got the car fixed. I did it myself but not before paying $50 for the diagnosis," he said. "The guy wanted to charge me $100."

"For what?"

"For the diagnosis. There was a sign on the garage wall that said the terms but I didn't see the sign. He called the police."

"You're joking! Jeez! What happened?"

"I told the cop ..."

"The cop?"

"Yeah the cop–that's the name isn't it?–I told him I was a tourist and couldn't read English much. I had to pay $50 in the end."

"Jeez, you nearly got arrested. No wonder you're annoyed. I'll get you a coffee. I bet you need one." I ordered an espresso at the bar and when I returned, he was still furious. "Here," I said giving him the coffee. I took out $25 from my purse.

"I don't want your money," he said.

"I know you don't but we're travelling together. I don't want you in a bad mood for the rest of the day." He put out his hand to take the money then stopped.

"No, I don't want it."

"Didn't we say we would share the costs? If I'd been with you at the garage, we would have given the mechanic the money together. You know we would have. Take it, I want us on an even keel." He took the money.

"Thanks buddy," he said.

"That doesn't sound right in French."

"I said it in English."

"It's the accent. First cop, now buddy … Jesus, I can't believe we've been on the road a few days and had the cops called already." I shook my head. "Let's try and cross the county line in peace." We didn't leave that Starbucks until 5 pm. I had spent the entire day there.

That evening, we drove across a disused railway line and were surprised to discover we were at the far reach of a vineyard. I pitched my tent between the rows of vines and for the first time Leo could see my little one person tent as it wasn't yet dark. It was grey with orange trim and had just one metallic spine to hold it up with tension held with ties and pegs. It was tall and wide at the head and narrow and small at the foot. It was a one person sleeping chamber.

"I like your tent," he said. He was impressed.

"I chose it carefully. No room for anyone else. It's one of those serious tents, the kind that walkers have."

"I like it. You chose well." It felt good to sleep amongst the vines that night.

A farmer approached in the morning, a friend of the winegrower. He told us we were lucky as his friend wouldn't have liked it if he'd found us.

I was comfortable in the Rust Bucket the following morning. I was being driven around by a maniac–true–but I didn't have other stresses like driving. I was free to watch the houses and the shops go by and the occasional pedestrian. It seemed liked Americans never went out for a stroll. Were they all watching TV? If you drive from house to mall and back again then you never meet anyone unless you plan it. You'll only plan to meet people like yourself. Telling someone in America they need to get out of the house more may just narrow their experience.

Sometimes back in London, I would leave my house in the morning for a coffee and my day would expand in a million directions because of all the people I'd run into and the events that came about. I liked that. I didn't have anyone but I had everyone. I came to understand and sympathise with the guy who struggled to walk with his dog and found out that he had been attacked with a blow to the head so he wasn't a hopeless loser or a drunk. He was a carpenter who had his life wrecked by violence. You don't know these things until you get out the door and give people time, the one thing I had plenty of. And think about this–outside of this space-time reality–there is no such thing as time. It's something that we created in order to exist in the material plane. On a million other planes, time doesn't exist. It's a fiction.

35

Today was a fruit day and we were driving to Shinn Estate Vineyards in the North Fork where most of Long Island's vineyards are. Shinn Estate was having a superabundant flowering, not just the vines but the clovers, dandelions, mustards, sorrels and chicories used as cover crops on the soil between the vines.

"What about the *terroir*?" I asked as we parked the car.

"They practice biodynamics here. All those cover crops make the vine roots dig deeper and become stronger. Not to mention all the insects and they've got their own honeybees as well." We poked our fingers around in the soil with the winemaker and as I looked up I saw a couple of happy chickens pecking between the vines. I was a happy chicken too. The soil was lush, like a forest floor.

We began tasting the *Brut Sparkling*. I was happy. I gave a little swirl, a little sniff and a little sip. I felt my heart beat with happiness. I was in America! With a gorgeous French sommelier! He was only twenty-nine! I was having a moment on this wonderful fruit day, a moment in time with wine. The little bubbles moussed their creamy pleasure directly onto my tongue and into my bloodstream. What would others be doing right now? Little Lilly, my beloved feline friend–do you miss me? Leo was in his element once more. He expressed delight that the wines were fermented with yeasts from the vineyard.

"You have closed the circle," he said to the winemaker. "Everything you use comes from right here, even the yeasts. And your cover crops ..."

"When the vine shares the soil with other plants, it has to dig deeper for nutrients. The struggle of the vine expresses itself in the grape and hence, the wine," said the winemaker.

"Alive but poor–that's what makes a great vineyard soil. It makes for great minerality."

"So that's why it tastes so good." I said.

Yes, it was all about the *terroir*, each wine with its own signature of time, place, soil, weather and human consciousness. The day you open the bottle and sip is unique, a never to be replaced experience to be drunk but never forgotten. A natural biodynamic and sparkling wine–there was nothing better. A *quantum blanc*.

We moved onto a rosé, the wine for love and then onto the most expensive wine I had tasted thus far in my life, a wondrous being, a 2007 *Clarity*. Black fruits and coffee. How I loved those coffee aromas.

He became talkative later in the car. "You know, I can walk into any wine bar in the world and I can make a friend when I tell them I'm a *sommelier* from France."

"You don't seem to even drink much of it," I said.

"I have a cellar in France. It's full of wine. I don't know what to do with it."

"Why don't you drink it?"

"Because of the married woman. She gave me all this wine. She was seducing me. The boss' wife. It couldn't have been worse. There were other women too but with her ... it went on for over two years."

"Jesus. You don't seem like someone who would do that."

"I know, I was a different person then. I was young and stupid."

"You could have had anyone."

"I had to leave the job in the end. It was a mess. And now I have all this wine and I don't know what to do with it."

"Why don't you auction it on eBay and give the money to charity or give it away to your friends? I'll have some too," I offered, helpfully.

"That's a good idea."

"You don't have to do it all in one go, if it's easier. One bottle at a time, like AA except not one day at a time, one bottle at a time."

"It's my guilty secret."

"Just give it away. It's not worth keeping if it tortures you."

We snuck onto another vineyard that night to sleep and the following morning, we visited the beach near Jamesport. Leo said, "I wanna go for a walk on my own. I need some space. I'll see you back here in half an hour."

We walked in opposite directions and I allowed the cool white sand beneath my feet and the breeze and the cobalt sky to hold me. My mind was confused. I had to lean into the experience. I didn't want to leave. Not because I wanted Leo but because I had come so far and spent so much money and effort to get there. I had to get the best out of it. My mind flitted between the Leo I knew and the Leo that was in front of me or, rather, not in front of me right now. He was beautiful.

Our days on Long Island had been relatively good after the initial outburst. I had learned something about wine and our relationship had settled on fairly uncommunicative.

"You're quite alone, aren't you?" he had said to me that morning in the car. We had never stopped for a full evening meal, mostly eating in the car or cooking up in a parking lot. I knew he was acting something out and I thought his time management was ridiculous. I said nothing. I could bail at any time. So far, so no bail.

I saw a man sitting on the sand dunes and said good morning but he didn't reply. I wondered if he was a wealthy banker. I turned around and couldn't see where Leo was in the distance and decided to make my way back.

He was at the car with his camping stove cooking up rice. We would stay awhile. There were public lavatories and a shower. He was generous with his food, always cooked enough for both of us.

He asked me as he was cooking: "Why are you on this trip? You want a relationship with me?"

"I've come for the adventure," I replied. My heart sank as I said it. "It's an opportunity. I've never done long-distance travel. I've come for the landscape and maybe I'll learn something about wine." He was silent for a while as he stirred the pot and dished up the rice.

"I tried your writing technique–it works. I'm getting faster," he said as he gave me a plate of rice. "Thanks buddy." I poured olive oil on the rice.

"Glad to be of help," I replied as I took a mouthful. This was his pattern–to block everything because he was threatened but later take things on board and be sweet about it. It was now his idea. He needed to feel he was in control of everything. I had rarely met anyone this difficult and intent on being displeasing. I don't think he was by nature unpleasant. He was popular at college, others would call him 'such a nice person.' He had become hard with me. I was dealing with a hard wall, a person who was giving nothing. No kindness. Not normal. I wondered at my ability to attract such an experience. These were my thoughts as I tucked into basmati rice *à la Leo*. And still I stayed.

We drove back along the Long Island Freeway west this time, back in the direction of New York City.

36

I lost count of the cars on the New Jersey Turnpike. I hated those freeways, they weren't free at all. We took a wrong turning and had to go back on ourselves before trying again, the traffic as menacing as death metal. The map was not the *terroir*. I had to take stock. Bad traffic or no, it seemed there were forces in the Universe out to get me. How could I turn them in my favour?

Laura McLove. What the hell are you doing with your life? Is this part of your plan? Laura McLove, what gives?

There I was stuck in a car with a man I barely knew nor now had much care for in a foreign country without insurance. I was forty-six and not getting any younger. I had a diploma in agriculture that I neither needed nor wanted. I was 5'8" with red hair, greying at the edges. I weighed sixty-three kilos. I didn't care about wine. I cared about getting drunk.

I didn't own a home, nor even a suitcase.

Universe, I said, because in those days I talked to the Universe all the time, what gives? Am I on the right path?

Give me a sign. I've followed my intuition. I've put 100% trust in you. Is this what you want? Will it all work out? Am I a writer or a fool? Is there a difference? I had a longing for fulfilment. Is this what drove me on? That psychic back in London had said you don't have to be so restless, Laura, write about it instead. Use your imagination instead.

Universe, give me some more years so I can make something of myself. Laura McLove, the writer. It'll take some time, Universe, but maybe you could throw a beautiful man in for good measure. I looked over to my left and seeing Leo at the wheel, I realised that the Universe had indeed delivered. It had a greater plan, a plan that I would never fully understand and that I could never control.

37

Later in the afternoon, we arrived at the Pfeiffer Centre in Chestnut Ridge. As it happened, Leo hit it lucky because this weekend, there was a two day biodynamic workshop for farmers-in-training from around the country. Leo said, "You can do what you like now. I'm gonna explore. I'll see you later." I went for a walk to the village and found the natural food store and I even went out to a bar on my own for a beer.

    The first night, we camped out in secret. Fortunately on the Saturday night there was a party on a farm nearby and I pitched my tent in full light and in peace. I was uncomfortable at the party but Leo was happy to be open and share and make out like I was his good friend on a research trip.

    On Sunday, I found Leo swimming in Pfeiffer's outdoor pool and my instinct was to go and join him but I judged he wanted to be alone and so I carried on my day of not doing anything in particular, in fact, waiting for Leo to swim, attend his workshops, relate and do what he liked so long as I kept out of the way.

    "Why didn't you come in for a swim? I saw you and you didn't come in," he said when I ran into him later.

    "You would have been angry and think I was clinging on to you, that's why not," I replied.

    "You're free to do what you like."

    Sunday evening and it had been pouring with rain since late afternoon. I waited in the car. There had been nothing to do but wait and read. I finished *Eat Pray Love* with irritation. I liked it but felt conned. After all that self-inflicted upheaval, the author got another guy. She got her happy ending. A nice, safe, happy ending.

Leo returned from class happy. I'm not sure what he wanted with all these visits. I was beginning to think he was plain nosey. So he could say he had seen it all. Ticked off. He could show off to his narcissistic pool of holy-moly lap dancers back at Emerson. Yes, that was it. I knew his plan. We drove north and as we crossed the Hudson in the rain, he began to talk.

I felt stifled and wanted to express my anger. Instead, I opened the window and let in the beautiful Upstate New York air. It was humid with rain, but the driving gave us some cold air. I don't remember what he said then but when he stopped, I closed the window. He started to talk again a few minutes later and I repeated the same action. I was angry. The window opening allowed me to see the glorious green view unobstructed by raindrops and condensation on the window. I decided I needed to express myself. I closed the window and I said to him in my best voice,"I need to tell you that I'm quite angry about the way you treated me this weekend."

"You're angry at how I've treated *you*. You've been behaving like an idiot!" What had I done? Me? "You ignored me and excluded me all weekend!" He shouted back.

"You could have come on the course if you wanted to! I'm not stopping you doing what you want and if you don't like it then you know what you can do! I don't want to have a relationship with you!"

"Then why did you invite me here? This is your nonsense, not mine. You didn't have to invite me in the first place!" I opened the car window to breathe. Outside was the beautiful rain and damp and lush air and we passed under one of those American bridges right out of the programme titles to *Cheers* and I loved it.

"Stop opening the window! Are you mad?"

"Mad. Me? Well isn't that the biggest cop out of all. A man calling a woman mad. Yeah, that one always sticks, doesn't it? That one always has the ring of truth."

"What do you know about truth? You don't even know who you are!"

"I'm Laura McLove. I'm a good person and I'm paying for half of this gas, by the way, in case you've forgotten."

"I haven't forgotten."

"I mean, what do you want from me? You invite me all the way to the New World for your bloody wines, but you've done nothing but push me away since I got here. I'm doing my best now back off!"

"You're just a whore."

"Oh fuck you! You're just a whore wine, yeah that's what you are Leo. A whore wine. A wine that tricks you first then drops you!"

"By the way, your feet stink."

I was aghast. My feet were indeed smelly. It was the cheap rubber sandals that were the problem. I wound down the window once more to let the violence, not to mention the malodorous feet, be transmuted into the air. When I could finally bear the cold air no longer I closed the window for good and turned on the radio. The Rolling Stones were having nineteen nervous breakdowns.

"I want off this trip. You have to take me to a train station to get back to New York," I said. Leo's mouth gawped as he stared at the road.

"We need somewhere to park." The rain had drizzled off and it was getting dark.

We drove along a side road then turned on to a little track, steep uphill into woods. The car was at a thirty degree gradient amongst wet leaves when Leo braked. We were hidden from the road below. I pitched my tent next to the car on the slope. There was no more point in arguing. I was crying but it was half forced and so I got in my tent but I couldn't settle. I got up to walk around and to talk to Leo who was by now trying to sleep in the back of the Saturn. He said, I want to sleep now. Leave it alone until tomorrow. I was distraught. I went for a walk. I pleaded with the Universe once more–give me a sign!

I walked up the hill on the crunchy undergrowth and came to a clearing. I saw bright red lights dashing everywhere. Fireflies! I'd never seen fireflies before. Tears came to my eyes until I pulled myself away, returned to my tent and entered a deep sleep.

I heard the car door open in the morning and yelled from inside my sleeping bag "I'm sorry!"

"What for?"

"For everything." I said, "I want to stay on this trip."

I crawled out of my tent to see Leo rubbing his teeth with a stick. "Does that actually work?" I asked.

"Of course it works."

"And that crystal that you use under your arms–does it stop the smell or the sweating?"

"It stops the smell. It's not natural to stop the sweat."

"I still buy the chemical stuff."

"You need it for your feet."

"Hey, don't sweat the small stuff. I'll deodorise my feet this morning," I said.

If you didn't buy stupid rubber shoes your feet wouldn't be so badass," said Leo.

"Badass? Badass? You're hilarious. For someone who's all *Monsieur Naturel* you seem to be so angry."

"I'm not angry. Angry at what?"

"Me. You're angry at me."

"I'm not angry at you. Your feet stink, that's all."

"You seem to be angry at me. You seem to be angry, full stop."

"I'm angry."

"I don't think you like women much. You think we're going to smother you. I say you've got mother issues."

"I like women but yeah, they do want to smother me. I need to be free to do what I want. *Je veux préparer mes sandwiches moi-même.*"

"What kind of answer is that? You want to make your own sandwiches? You're ridiculous!"

We got into the car once more and as I sat in the passenger seat I deodorised one foot at a time (sweet Jesus) rolling around the little ball of the deodorant first through my toes with the help of my fingers, then the sole. I crossed my leg and hung my foot in the air to dry and then rolled deodorant on top of my foot. I rolled the deodorant onto the rubber sandal too, just for good measure. It did the trick. And then the other foot.

"There! You're safe now," I said. "I don't think that crystal of yours would have been up to the job. You really are

Monsieur Naturel aren't you? Is that why you wear beige? Because it's natural?"

"No, it's just what I found."

"Your trousers are beige. Those cotton pickin' hemp pants that you insist on wearing."

"There's no bleach in them and they're really cool."

"They may keep you cool but they're not cool. I don't think you suit the hippy look, it's a waste of your looks. You're French, you're supposed to be chic."

"You just can't forget I'm French."

"I don't want to forget you're French. You need to make the most of your looks. You're hot, you could give it the *je ne sais quoi*."

"Are all Scottish people like you?"

"My family's Irish by the way, it might explain the blarney."

"What's the blarney?"

"It's a stone. It's a castle. If you kiss it, it gives you the gift of conversation."

"Have you kissed it?"

"Yeah and I'm gonna kiss you in a minute."

"Well if it gets you to shut up."

38

Leo, me and my now deodorised feet arrived at yet another biodynamic place to a community at Copake. It was glorious. We pitched up by the 'swim-lake', a small pond with a wooden sauna hut on its little shore. A cafe here with wifi allowed Leo to blog away happily. The American biodynamic calendar I found in the bookshop said it was a root day. Not best for drinking wine.

After a quick swim, Leo drove to town for more blogging at another cafe. I lingered on my own around the tent and enjoyed some peace. It was a whole lot easier to feel relaxed when your bed for the night was secure. Still, I had a residual anxiety about when Leo would return. I got into my tent at dusk and settled. As night fell, I began to hear a strange noise and then another. A whole chorus of bullfrogs wishing me goodnight. Then I heard a car and it felt good to know Leo was back.

At 3 am, the time between worlds, I awoke in a kind of torment. I heard a drop of water so loud and I wondered where it came from. It wasn't raining anymore, there was no pit-a-pat on the tent. Then silence. I heard a second drop of water, louder and wider somehow. It was behind me. It was in the tent. Then there was a third, this time though there was also a voice. It was a woman's voice, soft and hushed, not recognisable to me as anyone I had ever known. Just one syllable I heard with the soft plop of the raindrop falling into a pool and the voice said,

'LOVE'

Another drop of water was coming. I tucked my head into my sleeping bag and asked it to stop. There were no more drops of water but as I closed my eyes, my mother's face came to me, right before my eyes then quickly faded backwards into the dark.

Unzipping the tent in the morning, the first thing I saw was the back of a naked man standing by the pool. I stared at his buttocks and took in the fresh morning air and the blue sky and birds and trees rustling until he dived in. I lay down again and heard him swim about and move around and then he went into the sauna. I got up as usual with the sound of the car door opening. Leo also went for a swim although sadly it wasn't a naked one. The naked man came out of the sauna with clothes on, introduced himself as John and invited us for breakfast.

People were impressed with Leo. He was beautiful and eager to learn. He could go real quiet sometimes in awe of the person he was around and project a mystique onto them. He introduced himself to John as a farmer's son and called his farm back in Bordeaux 'his' farm although it was his parents'. We drank coffee and ate waffles with maple syrup as John told us of his plan to single-handedly row down the Hudson to New York City and row back up again on the East River this year. He invited us again for breakfast the following morning to see us off.

We spent a pleasant day visiting Hawthorne Valley farm in Ghent although I was wearying of talking about biodynamics and acting interested. It was hard work, something to which I had a lifelong aversion.

39

The next day after more coffee, waffles and maple syrup we began our drive to the Finger Lakes, further upstate. Our first stop was at a library in a deserted two horse town. Many of the Finger Lakes towns had an abandoned air. Leo logged on the internet whilst I read *The New York Times*. I thanked the American public mentally for letting us log on to their networks when we didn't even have a library ticket.

We drove down to Seneca Lake by evening and found a picnic spot, empty and peaceful, the lake still. At a wooden bench and table we tucked into some of our goodies from Hawthorne Valley shop–rye bread and cheddar, raw vegetables and nuts. The sun was setting. "I think we should sleep here," said Leo. "There's showers and we could have a swim in the morning. We'll just have to sit here until it's nearly dark." Unlike at Long Island when much of the ocean was off-limits with mansions or paying beaches, we could linger and enjoy the view. We were the only picnickers left.

At dusk. Leo manoeuvred the Rust Bucket to a spot near some trees and I pitched the tent beneath low growth and climbed in after saying goodnight. It was strange and I was a little nervous but soon I was off to sleep.

Voices and bright light woke me. I listened for a moment. The light shone right through the tent. The voices were coming from the direction of Leo's car. If he was taken away in the night I would wake up all alone in America.

I pulled on some clothes and unzipped the tent to find a black police car with two open front doors and its full headlights parked right in front of the Rust Bucket. Leo was standing in the spotlight and I walked towards him. The night was clean and clear. It was 2 am.

"You should have stayed in your tent," he said. "They can't see you over there."

"We're in this together," I replied, "I don't want to wake up in the morning and you're gone."

I didn't admit that this would be my worst nightmare. To get up out of my tent in the morning and no car, no Leo.

"They took my passport," he said. A police officer got out of the police car and said, "Are you camping over there?"

"Yes," I replied. "Do you want to see my passport too?"

"No, that won't be necessary." He returned to the police car.

"They asked me if I had been drinking," said Leo. "They don't know what to make of me. I've got visas for Iran, India and Afghanistan. They don't understand why I'm sleeping in my car and I'm not drinking. They probably think I'm French Canadian."

"They think you're a hobo," I said. "Which you are, in a way. They're probably checking you're not on some 'most wanted' list. You might end up in Guantanamo. I hope you haven't got a copy of the Insurgents' Handbook in the trunk."

Leo strode towards the police car and lobbied for his passport. He had no sense of humility or politeness and the belligerence was magnified by a French accent. Sorry officer, I wanted to say, my friend doesn't understand Anglo American culture. He's French.

One of the police officers returned with Leo. "We're not going to disturb you as it's the middle of the night, but please get up and leave early in the morning," he said.

"Thank you officer. I appreciate that," I replied.

After the drama, more sleep and we got up before 7 am and drove off.

40

Silver Thread winery near Lodi on the east side of Seneca Lake was our first visit. The entrance was along a country lane. A neighbour had posted a sign 'This Is Not a Winery' at their gate so it wasn't *that* turning. We took the correct turning and a dark wooden hut with a roof sloping to the ground presented itself. For the first time, I relaxed into the visit. A beautiful tasting room overlooked the lake with the winery downstairs.

It was a fruit day, a good day, a sunny day, a great day for tasting, a super day in my life. Me and the Frenchman were getting along swimmingly. We sipped and listened and swallowed and spat. Chardonnay, Gewurztraminer, Riesling, Pinot Noir, Cabernet Franc. I loved these temperate climate whites. My untrained palate bought a bottle of Gewurztraminer 2007. Leo loved Silver Thread and the winemaker said yes to our request to come back to camp for the night later.

Silver Thread inspired Leo. "That's exactly what I want when I make my own wine –a *petit domaine*, working biodynamically, selling from the winery, small enough to manage without too much stress. It's perfect, one of the best I've seen."

"I'm looking forward to camping there tonight," I said. "Maybe we can open the Gewurztraminer?"

"You picked the best one! Well done buddy!"

"Praise indeed! So I'm learning something at last!"

We had a second appointment two miles south at Standing Stone Vineyards after a lunch in the car. There was a much cleaner and emptier feel to the Finger Lakes than Long Island. More moisture in the air, cleaner with less traffic and for the first time we saw Amish buggies on the road. The lake water looked pure and fresh. This change of air was serving us well.

Standing Stone is a commercial enterprise with a large, sage-green tasting room in a converted barn. Upright wine barrels acted as tasting tables. We tasted the full 'flight' of their wines– twelve in all. I was quiet but I listened intently. Swilling, sniffing and sipping more Riesling, Gewurztraminer, Merlot, Pinot and Cabernet Sauvignon.

The two of us made a strange pair. We toured the vines with a young man called Hank, poking our fingers in the soil. I spied chickens again and there was a pond of orange carp, as bright as my hair.

41

We emerged from that winery in an alcoholic funk. Some of the day's wine couldn't help but get in the bloodstream. There was no tension anymore between us. The car had been sitting in the sun and it was now blisteringly hot inside and out. Leo was desperate for a swim. I wondered if the incident with the police had affected his opinion of me for better or worse. Certainly, I had shown loyalty and calmness under stress.

We drove back to Silver Thread, past the winery and along a lane parallel to the vines downhill. Leo wanted the lake. We turned right onto a steeper incline through a wood and then a hairpin bend took us down steeper and further. We were off vineyard land now. The lake was in sight, dappling beneath the trees and I said "I'm going to go skinny-dipping."

"What's skinny dipping?"

"It's swimming naked, that's what it is."

"That might not be a good idea," he said.

"It's something I've never done and I want to do it once in my life and if it feels right, I'm going to do it."

We stopped at a scaffolding platform with a ladder that led down to the lakeside. We changed into swimming gear at the car and climbed down. There was no-one. Leo walked to the door of a nearby wooden chalet and knocked. He knocked again–no reply. He said, "There's no-one in. We can swim."

The lake was blue and clean with a slight lapping on the shore. It must have been around six with the sun lower in the sky casting its orange glow. I made sure to swim a distance from Leo so as not to threaten him. It was the time. It was now. I knew it had been a special day of my life and I pulled off my black swimsuit under the water. I waved it in a circle in the air. "Woohoooo! I've done it!" I said and threw the costume onto the shore.

Liberated at last, I was liberated. I was cool and cold and free and light and it was fantastic. I swam on my front and I swam on my back and it was beyond anything I had expected. Leo shouted, "I'm gonna play that game too!" as he took off his trunks, waved them in the air and threw them on the shore.

He had already seen me naked so that hadn't worried me, in fact, it liberated me to skinny-dip. I was far enough away from him for it not to be overtly sexual. I enjoyed and so did he this liberation, together but apart. There were a couple of boats passing in the distance but both of us swam and splashed apart from each other delighting in it. I was happy he had relaxed. There was sun and lake and wine and freedom and we were on holiday. He was beautiful and he told me later, so was I.

He got out of the lake first and stood naked before me on the shore. I tried not to be overt about looking. I relaxed, looking and not looking until I noticed that he was excited. *Interesting*, I thought ... I waited until he had covered himself before I got out. Drying off with my back to him, I turned my head to find him staring. He was rapt. He had been looking at me that way for a while.

We climbed the scaffolding again and started the car. Past the hairpin bend, we halted. It was too steep. The Rust Bucket groaned, stopping and starting next to a sheer drop down. I began to panic. "I'm gonna have to reverse and take the hill as fast as I can. You need to get out. I can't have you screaming, you'll go nuts," he said. He wasn't angry, he was matter-of-fact and he was right. "Happy to oblige," I replied and got out of the car. I wondered if we would ever get the car off this road.

Leo reversed down the dirt track back to the hairpin and stopped. He restarted and raced up the hill with a couple of chokes. The old Rust Bucket and Leo did good. We were back on vineyard land.

I wedged the bottle of Gewurztraminer in a tiny stream at the edge of the vineyard to chill whilst I put up the tent and sorted out our belongings for the night and prepared some food. The sun was still setting over the lake.

Leo opened the wine and I said to him, "This was the best day." And I meant it. "It was the best day, one of the best days of my life. Ever."

"Thanks for showing me skinny-dipping. You looked beautiful swimming. I wanted to try it too."

He took out two Riedel glasses, polished them with a cloth and held them up to the setting sunlight then poured us a glass each of the now chilled Gewurztraminer. He placed his glass on the car roof and took a photograph with the orange light of the setting sun streaming through the glass with the lake in the background. He put the photo on his blog. You can still see it there. He laughed and said he had taken a photo of me skinny-dipping and that he would put that on his blog too.

I was so happy and the wine was so good and we had a great place to camp, the best campground in all of north America and my little tent was on an incline so I would have a good sleep with my head higher than my deodorised toes. After fun and talking I wondered if he would make a pass at me but he never did. Never mind. I was happy. A good day. A good swim. A good wine. A good sleep. A perfect day, just like Lou Reed sang. I was beginning to reap what I'd sown.

Next morning, we woke early and the sun was shining on the lake. "It is quite special to camp out on a vineyard," said Leo. We'd become closer to the vines and could understand the peace of the place. We were breathing the same air as the leaves and the grapes and the insects and had drunk the wine from the same soil and air and climate. The *terroir*, in fact. We had slept in the *terroir*. Now our energy was part of the *terroir*. We'd become the *terroir*.

Leo asked me, "How do you feel this morning?"
"Good," I said.
"That's how you should feel after a good wine. No headaches, just clarity. No sulphur."

We ate and peed and packed and drove off. We were headed to the other side of the lake for another two visits tomorrow—one squeezed in at the last minute—but for today, it was time for blogging and we were headed back south.

We stopped at a little town and found a diner. Leo was walking in front of me for a moment until he turned and waited. "I know you don't like it," he said.

"It's nice to know that you don't want to walk in front of me now," I said.

The diner was big with lots of people in and had a long bar and we took a cubicle seat by the window. We ate eggs on toast and gratin potatoes. And coffee, of course. Oh, how I love diner coffee in America–here's always a free top-up.

"I've often had girlfriends who were older than me," said Leo.

"Have you?" I said. I wondered at the workings of his mind. Seeing me skinny-dip had shifted something in him.

42

The day was hot and sticky. We were headed for Watkins Glen at the head of Seneca Lake. We drank the breeze, windows open, speeding along near its shore. Rust Bucket, I salute you now!

Three women were playing fiddle, banjo and double bass at the town square. At a little farmers' market, I bought some white New York cheddar from a boy with his dad, both of them dressed in jeans and red checked shirts.

We sat on a bench under trees in earshot of the bluegrass and Leo opened his netbook. I offered to type for him because he was so slow and for the first time I felt we were working together. He could just speak what he wanted to write and I typed it down. He was happy. I was happy.

Next he needed the internet. We arrived at the local library an hour before closing. I picked up a *New York Times* and sat in an armchair. I was happy. Again. Later, I went to the bookshelves and pulled out a book with my eyes closed. I held the book to my chest and asked The Universe a question—what was to become of me? I opened the book at random and placed my finger in the text. I read:

'Come along Toto,' she said. 'We will go to the Emerald City and ask the great Oz how to get back to Kansas.'

I fell back into the armchair. A lonely wave of emotion crashed on the shore of my fragile heart. There was no place like home. I wanted to cry. Instead, I pulled out my new notebook and a pen and I started to write. The sad words flowed freely but didn't make sense. Carlos Castaneda said to be free you have to give up your story. But I wasn't at that moment of complete freedom yet, I was in a moment of choosing my future, still in search of my story.

I was a nomad. Borderless with the world, it existed in me and without me, like a memory of an indigenous past. Was this happiness? Did I already own it? Was that it? I could read nature, I could read Spirit. I had the faith. I knew it. That was all I needed. No man, no job, no money, in an eternal present in my body, connected with everything. I had access to an innate intelligence, the one before the Text got control.

It was all about control. Western civilisation, just like a revolution, was eating itself. It was all about control instead of all about love which was all you needed anyway.

I knew why I hated jobs–everyone did. Civilisation depended on compulsory labour, a domestication, a sublimation of who we were and then we were told that we enjoyed it. It was a lie and we knew deep down we had enslaved ourselves, we had given our power away. My personal traumas were the traumas of civilisation itself. The Powers That Shouldn't Be masqueraded in front of our faces now and still we didn't act. We were tigers in a cage, asleep.

The lonely hour, the hour of malcontents, the dispossessed, the fractured and the broken, was over quickly in the library. Leo and I walked back to the car, located our first winery for the following day, found a place to park up for the night a few miles away, said our goodnights and went to our separate beds.

43

A winemaker is a romantic. It took a special dedication to the land. It was farming after all, with hard graft in all weathers, the diseases, the pruning, the tractors, the harvest. Why would you let two wayfaring tourists spend the night on your precious vineyard? Why not? was the response. It was like they wanted us there.

We walked out onto the Nutt vineyard of Anthony Road Winery with the winegrower. We were poking our fingers in the soil once again as Leo did the talking. I stood up and looked towards that wondrous Lake Seneca and was renewed once more. I was so familiar with looking at places, at scenery. I was now becoming familiarised with the taste of places, the taste of a place, the concept of *terroir*. Wine was neither all natural nor all cultural, a bottle of wine was man-made. A beautiful wine expressed the relationship between nature and culture, between the sun and the moon, the soil and the vine and its fruit–and the labour, artistry and skill of the vine-grower and winemaker.

A natural wine is purer, wilder, unknowable until you open the bottle. A brilliant wine, or a poor one, completely different from one year to the next, changeable like the weather, unmanageable therefore, and like a child. The biodynamic method engaged more living energy from the cosmos to the soil, vine and grape and the natural method in the winery meant that it was not just a living thing, but a spiritual being. An expression not just of the *terroir,* an expression of the All That Is, the energy that creates worlds. And it got you pissed. And here's the thing–no sulphur, no hangover.

Back at the winery on Anthony Road, another tasting. Swirling, sniffing and sipping whilst I listened in to the conversation between Leo and the winemaker. Leo was impressed with the soft, sweet wines here and the Vignoles, a wine made from a French-American hybrid grape. We were given a gift of a 2005 Pinot Gris.

We wandered out to the garden later and sat on a bench overlooking the lake. How strange it seemed to me that a landscape this beautiful and close to a world trading centre, was so little populated with some towns left almost abandoned.

The Rust Bucket had become an oven once more and we drove quickly towards shade to eat in the car before a last visit on the lakes at Herman J Wiemer. We started off the tasting much to my happiness with a sparkler, *Cuvée Brut 2006*.

Back to Nutt Road vineyard at evening and I pitched up on the slope next to the vines. The best campground of all–an organic vineyard with a view over water. We camped in tranquillity as the sun set over Seneca Lake.

44

Leo was obsessed now with naked swimming. We were at French Creek near Phoenixville, Pennsylvania, having driven all day on the interstate from New York. We were visiting an estate of four hundred glorious acres of woodland, gardens and farmland but we were early for the person Leo was meeting and he wanted to refresh from the driving.

The Creek was pebbly and shallow and sheltered by trees. I took my smelly feet and waded in with my trousers rolled up to test the water. It was cold. Dipping in with underwear on at first, I then took off my bra. Leo took off all his clothes and propped himself up on the stones, allowing his body to float. The sun-dappled water rippled over his naked body and rippled over mine.

We kept half an eye on each other in that nervous way, pretending we weren't so excited by it all, to be naked in nature. A couple of cars passed on the bridge nearby and one of them had kids laughing. They were far enough away but it was then I decided to get out and dried myself whilst watching Leo still enjoy the water.

They were special moments when Leo was happy although I kept my distance. The idle moments passed and soon enough we were in the car looking for somewhere to eat.

We stopped at a bar and as we perched on stools for beer and fries, I noticed there were three TVs on—one for sports behind the bar, one high up on the wall to the right with a reality game show and another high up to the left with MTV. It was the music that had the volume up, the other two were silent. We drank our beer, ate some fries and left.

No more wine from now on, but more earnestness about land and farming. I took a back step and let Leo enjoy his research and I enjoyed a few days walking, reading and camping.

A curious thing happened whilst we were here that befuddled me for a while afterwards. Leo wanted to shower with me. Skinny-dipping had opened up a portal in his mind. We went indoors to one of the communal buildings and locked ourselves in a large bathroom. Leo switched on the shower and stepped in and then so did I. He reached to touch me and I reached to touch him back, but I wasn't sure what he wanted and he was nervous and in the end we both had separate showers and left and later I sat in the car, confused.

"I don't know what you want," I said.

"I don't think it's a good idea. We shouldn't do this. I don't want a relationship," he replied.

"We have one whether you want it or not." I gave it up. At least I was clean.

We visited Kimberton Whole Foods in the village as we were leaving and as Leo went to the cafe for the wifi, I wandered around looking at the local ads, newspapers, cards, jewellery, all those things for the wholesome hippy traveller. I loved shops like this. I joined Leo for coffee later but he was writing away on his blog. I returned to the shop and bought coffee, cheese, oatcakes and peanut butter and waited for him in the car. He arrived with a huge box of food.

"How come you bought so much?" I asked.

"I didn't buy anything! I told them I was a farming student on a tour of the US and did they have anything near the sell-by date and they gave me all of this!"

At lunchtime we stopped at a parking lot and I ate a wrap with 'natural' chicken and shuddered at the thought of what an 'unnatural' chicken might be like. Still, we were grateful for so much and it was the kind of food we would never have bought for ourselves–all the cook-chill stuff, salads and sandwiches and wraps and all that plastic packaging.

We continued south on the I-81. We were headed for Woolwine, Virginia.

45

At around four o'clock, Leo took the high road onto the Blue Ridge Parkway. It was an impulsive decision but a good one. We met barely a car in the late afternoon as we drove through woods. Driving higher and higher, out of the woods now and onto the Ridge with clear blue skies, blue peaks and valleys as far as we could see. Wow.

"Why would anyone live in a city when you can have this?" Leo asked. I couldn't answer. I was stupefied by beauty. It was silent at Irish Creek Valley where we stopped and stood to watch the sunset. We were at 2,600 feet.

I turned on the radio back in the car.

"It's nice, I like that music. What is it Laura?"

"I don't know, for once," I said. "It's lovely though. What does it make you think of?"

"I dunno."

"Try. If it was a wine …?"

"Burgundy."

"Ha! from the Côte d'Or! Is it oaked?"

"Yeah–in old barrels. The Californians are crazy for French oak."

"Why would it be oaked?"

"To get the nuance of the flavour. This music has depth. Have you heard it before?"

"It's familiar, but I don't know why." We were quiet for a time, looking out at the landscape.

"So it's not a champagne then?" I persisted.
"No."
"How does it make you feel?"
"Quiet."
"Yeah, it makes me quiet too."
"Then why are you asking so many questions?"

We didn't pass another car that evening. At dusk, we found a parking space surrounded by woodland and as Leo parked the car, the radio announced we had been listening to *Adagio For Strings* by Samuel Barber. I pitched my tent on the greenery nearby with the Rust Bucket obscuring me from the road, as usual. No cars passed.

We woke before seven on top of the mountain in the sun. I saw an eagle high in the sky as Leo boiled water and began to wash himself. He asked me if I wanted a wash too so I stood naked in the open air with him standing over me giving me a little rinse once from time to time, and after shampooing my hair, he poured the rest of the warm water all over me from top to toe. He began boiling more water as I dressed then I took over for making coffee, cowboy style. My technique involved adding two tablespoons of coffee and stirring, then returning the coffee to the heat a couple of times without letting it boil. I loved the novelty of it. I poured the coffee into cardboard cups saved from the last coffee stop on the road, added creamer and one sugar each. We drove off windows down, drinking coffee. Happiness was ours. I started to sing:

> "She'll be comin' round the mountain when she comes
> She'll be comin' round the mountain when she comes
> She'll be comin' round the mountain,
> comin' round the mountain,
> comin' round the mountain when she comes"

Leo was smiling. I began again:

> "She'll be wearing pink pyjamas when she comes
> She'll be wearing pink pyjamas when she comes
> She'll be wearing pink pyjamas, wearing pink pyjamas,
> wearing pink pyjamas when she comes"

"You've got a good voice Laura," said Leo.

"I once played in a band called *Pennsylvania Mania*. Would you believe it? We sang Gene Autry, old cowboy songs. We only ever did one gig. It was a good one too. We were all dressed up in cowboy gear. I love that cowboy shit."

"Why did you only do one?"

"We did it for a laugh. There was just me and three other guys. They did three part harmony. I played the accordion."

I started to sing: "Back in the saddle again …" but I couldn't remember all the words.

"I can't remember all the words. Why don't you sing something Leo?"

"I'm not a singer."

"There must be something. How about *Je Ne Regrette Rien*?"

"*Non*," he replied. He was quiet for a moment then began to sing The Beatles, "Michelle …" in French. It was lovely. He was beautiful to me once more.

When he finished I said, "I thought you didn't know about music?"

"Everyone knows The Beatles though, don't they? Even I know a little bit of The Beatles."

"I love your French accent."

"I'm French." He shrugged. "What do you want to get out of America, Laura?" he asked.

"A cowboy hat. I'd like a cowboy hat. I love cowboys, I'd like to have sex with a cowboy. If I find a cowboy hat, you …"

"OK. A cowboy hat. This cowboy music, is that your favourite music, then?"

"I like music played by Gypsies."

"Gypsy music."

"No, not Gypsy music. Gypsy music doesn't exist. I said I like music played by Gypsies."

"That's *bizarre*." He pronounced it in French.

"Gypsy music doesn't exist. In France, a Gypsy might play swing … in Spain, flamenco. Japanese play Beethoven these days, does that make Beethoven Japanese?"

"No."

"If you take up the sitar, does that make you Indian? Does it make the sitar French?

"No but I'm not gonna be a musician. I'm gonna be a winemaker and a farmer."

"You play Indian music on your computer," I continued. "You're not from India," I said. "If I liked bluegrass–actually I do like bluegrass–you wouldn't bat an eyelid and I'm not American. Mind you, it has Scottish and Irish roots ... I like pop music too. I like Madonna. I like *Ray of Light*."

"Yeah *Ray of Light*." He was nodding his head thoughtfully. "Remind me not to ask you about music again."

"Did you ever see any films by Tony Gatlif? He lives in Paris."

"No, I haven't."

"He's Roma, a Gypsy. His first film has no dialogue, it's a travelogue of music along the trail of where the Gypsies came from and where they travelled to–all the way from Rajasthan to France. You'd love it."

"I went to Rajasthan."

"That's so cool!"

"I loved it, I love India. So Gypsies come from India?"

"They left Rajasthan because they were the lowest caste. It's right up your street. There are no greater travellers than Gypsies."

"We were all nomads before farming began, it's what we have now that's unnatural. It's normal, and it's ecological too, to move around and not deplete the soil."

"You're all about the soil, the *terroir*."

"*Le terroir, c'est moi*. We need to be building soil, there's only so much of it to grow our food on."

"I love your passion for farming. Not sure about the transatlantic flights this time around though, even for me. God you know what?"

"What?"

"That psychic said I was a channel."

"What psychic?"

"The psychic I went to see at the school. Apparently I'm channelling music. That's what she said. Anytime there's a problem, I can quiet my mind and ask for a song so when one pops up–it's the answer."

"So, what's the song for this trip?" he asked.

"*America*, Simon and Garfunkel. That's obvious."

We passed an older man, a hiker on his own clambering up through the woods from the Appalachian Trail onto the road. We slowed for a deer by the roadside–hello fragile beauty–and watched her so close to our car, the high view and mountains behind. We passed no other cars.

Just before Rocky Knob, we took the exit at Tuggle Gap onto Woolwine Highway.

46

Oh how I was fed up with biodynamics and farming! At the Josephine Porter Institute in Woolwine they make biodynamic preparations for the whole of America. You ought to really make your own but ... enough of biodynamics.

We headed off to Floyd on the Friday night following a tip off from the Institute's son Paul. We drove back along Woolwine Highway then onto Parkway Lane South until we arrived at a crossroads with the Crooked Road music trail. Friday night was playing in the street night. Violins, banjos, guitars, mandolins, double basses, singing, flat foot dancing. Floyd was alive to bluegrass and mountain music. We met Paul at the Dogtown Roadhouse and ordered Blue Mountain Lagers and wood-fired pizzas and sat outside in the evening sun, music everywhere. After one beer, Leo went off for a wander. Paul and I stayed for another beer. Paul reckoned that if the Pope knew about biodynamics, he'd say, "This is the shit!"

"I don't think he'd put it quite like that," I replied. He asked me if I was in a relationship with Leo, "I've been wondering all day," he said.

"Leo's too old for me."
"What age is he?"
"Twenty-nine."
"And what age are you?"
"Forty-six," I replied.
"Respect!" We high fived.

Leo had a mood on during the drive back. A woman had offered him a room for the night. It was my fault he couldn't take it.

At Floyd again the following day, Leo and I went separate ways. I found myself at the library, going online and having a coffee. Libraries that served coffee? Revolutionary.

Next day, next stop–Spikenard Farm Honeybee Sanctuary in Little River Valley ten miles north-east of Floyd. We stopped at a garage for a few hours to change and buy two new tyres–not the best way to spend a day but the RB needed the TLC.

47

The honeybee sanctuary was hidden on Hideaway Lane and after our arrival in the late afternoon, we began work on its garden as a gesture towards our host, Wolfgang. It was a delightful piece of land. Surrounded by pastures and forest and home to thirty quirky-shaped hives, each with their own name. Chickens, vegetables, wildflowers and an adjacent field planted with sunflowers, clover, mustard and other bee forage. We were free to camp out for the night and use the little wooden hut with its porch if we wished. Wolfgang pointed in the direction of Little River and said, "Maybe you like skinny-dipping?" Leo and I shared a glance.

Later, Wolfgang left to go home for dinner with his wife. I set about preparing a meal. I switched on a little radio and found Chopin's *Prelude in C Minor*. A red checked tablecloth already lay on the porch table. I brought out food from the car–rye bread, Virginia cheddar, mixed nuts, olive oil, hummus, tortilla chips, tomatoes, cucumber and, much to my delight, I discovered we still had the Anthony Road Pinot Gris. 'Banana and floral notes in the nose, with hints of apple, pear and gooseberry,' it said on the label.

"The moon's in my sign today," I called to Leo. "That means it's a fruit day. Sagittarius is a good sign for drinking wine."

I lay the table with plates and two of Leo's wine glasses. As it was getting dark, I found some tea light candles and lit them. I poured us both a drink and we clinked glasses. The stars were becoming visible. The food tasted like all great food tastes on warm summer nights eating outdoors–fabulous.

"What do you think of the wine Leo?"

"I think we're a perfect match," he said.

"I agree. This is bliss. Heaven. God, look at that sky! No wonder the bees do well here. It's a sanctuary for everybody."

"Look at that moon," said Leo. "It's huge. It's really close to the earth. It must be at perigee." I turned around to look and knocked into the table, spilling tea light wax everywhere.

"You've ruined the tablecloth! What have you done?!" yelled Leo.

"Oh God! What a mess!" I immediately put out all the candles. I was so stupid. I shouldn't be using other people's things without permission. I wanted to make it a lovely evening. There were so few when we had down-time. Everything had to be all my fault. This time it was. The night was becoming black and starlit and I had ruined it. My entire personality was up for grabs and all I could say was, "I'm sorry. It was a mistake."

"What am I gonna tell Wolfgang?" yelled Leo.

"That you've got a really stupid friend and that it's all my fault," I said. "I'll buy him another tablecloth and send it to him. I'm sorry. I shouldn't have done it. It wasn't deliberate. It's just a tablecloth. It's done now. It was a mistake." Leo went quiet and sipped more wine. Chopin played on in the background. At last, he announced, "I wanna go for a swim."

Nightfalling, we walked down Hideaway Lane then across a field in the direction of the river. Leo took off his clothes and went in. I did the same. The moon was enormous.

I moved through the water towards him and kissed his chest. The water felt and looked thick like black treacle, we couldn't see beyond its surface. A car passed on a nearby road. I wrapped my legs around him whilst holding his waist and he penetrated me in the water. I lay back and stared at that moon. A few minutes later another car drove in the opposite direction.

We returned to the porch of the little hut and Leo laid out some towels on the floor and switched on the radio. We undressed–still wet–but the radio was crackling. He was butt naked as he bent over to adjust it until finally he gave up and turned it off. We made hot, wet love under the still moon.

He wanted to sleep separately as usual and woke in the car happy, he said the next morning. I pretended to be happy but in fact I was confused.

I spent an hour exhausting myself removing candle wax from that pesky tablecloth. I boiled a kettle and used it like an iron. I found brown paper and put it between the cloth and the kettle surface. With repeated rubbing of the paper and cloth along the side, the wax melted onto the paper as the water boiled. With more and more paper and repeated boilings of water, I removed almost all the wax so that now it was only visible if you held the cloth up to the sunlight. I had done a good job but I was hot and sweating from the task.

Leo left a note for Wolfgang. I expect it said something like: "Thank you Wolf for this lovely night camping here. I'm afraid to say I'm travelling with an idiot who managed to stain your lovely tablecloth with tealight wax. It was nothing to do with me. I am perfect." We left the sanctuary mid-morning. His mood was sunny as the day.

48

A couple of hours later, Leo swerved suddenly into a side road and braked hard by a stream. It was quiet but for the sound of the water. It was a beautiful spot–trees, a fresh little breeze, dappled light on the stream. I looked up to the sky through the trees and saw a scarlet bird perched on a branch.

It was the birds I noticed first when I moved to the country. I thought of the Hopi, the Arapaho, the Blackfoot Indians destroyed in the wake of Columbus. They would have heard the birdsong, our first gift on earth from the longest lasting creature living longer than the dinosaurs. The birds had survived that great meteor strike and they were here for one reason alone, beyond eternity, just to sing. The blackbird, the nightingale, they would outlive us and it's what we forgot in our rush for stuff, in our violence we forgot to simply look at the day and sing. It was our primal auditory experience. Birds. It's what they do, stupid. They sing.

I returned my gaze to Leo–maybe he wanted to pee? He looked back and said, "I wanna cook."

He opened the trunk of the car and took out his Nepal camping stove, fired the gas canister and created a flame. I had a pee and paddled in the stream to relieve my smelly feet then watched whilst he cooked basmati rice with herbs, then adding sea salt and olive oil.

"I love cooking outdoors. It makes me feel independent, like I'm in control," he said.

"You are in control," I said. You're a rugged individualist, a man of the road."

He served up two bowls of rice and proceeded to pour tomato ketchup in his own bowl and stirred it all together. "God, you really are eating a big plate of crazy for lunch. I thought you French adored good food."

"This is how they do it in India," he replied.

"It looks like *malbouffe* to me."

"Where did you hear that word for junk food? I never heard an English person use it."

"Come on, I'm a Francophile, and just for the akashic record, I'm not English. How can you eat junk when you're all about the *terroir*? How in God's name can you eat rice with ketchup? I mean, don't you have a sensitive palate?"

"I told you, it's what they eat in India. I love it."

"It's what *you* ate in India. I understand they eat curry there."

"They eat basmati rice. I'm just giving it extra flavour. I don't care, I like junk food, I like *malbouffe*."

"You are the *roi de crazy*. The king of crazy shit." I was a lady who lunched on rice, no ketchup.

49

West Virginia, Indiana, Illinois, Wisconsin.

Somewhere in Indiana, we spent another night in a parking lot, camping up in the dark. His temper was bad. I could still hear traffic from the freeway but, worse, I could hear a horse. I was up earlier than Leo in the morning–I could hear a man and a horse. I was relieved when I got up–the horse was nowhere to be seen. I was also embarrassed. I'd just spent the night in a parking lot.

When Leo awoke, I said, "I'm buying you breakfast this morning. I need decent cooked food after last night."

"You're always trying to buy me off," came his reply.

At an Amish diner we ate eggs, hash browns, bacon, toast and plenty of filter coffee. I began to feel normal again.

Leo struck up a conversation with the waitress. She mentioned an Amish farmer and horseman nearby who was happy to work with non-Amish and Leo decided to meet him. That day, we visited our first Amish farm equipment factory. Everything you could ever want for a horse. I was weary. Especially when I heard we would be returning this way by the weekend for an agricultural show.

The Amish Horse Days ought to have been fun because the parking and camping were free and the weather was sunny. We had been as far as Wisconsin for more biodynamic meets, now back to Topeka, Indiana for a horse equipment fair.

Leo wanted to be alone and do his own thing so I lost him and found myself wandering aimlessly and staring at farming contraptions. Thoreau's book *Walden* came to mind as I watched an Amish team erecting a wooden cabin. Thoreau had built, then lived in, a cabin on Walden Pond to learn to 'live deep'. The land was owned by his friend Emerson. I'd also built a home on Emerson land but mine was on a landscape of the mind. I'd heard that different drummer. I'd stepped to that music and here I was, very far away indeed. I resolved to build my own cabin one day.

I wandered into Topeka. I found an Amish restaurant and had a bacon sandwich and coffee. I went to the library where I saw Amish on the internet and I saw another coming out of a car. I was bored.

Evening came and I got into my tent and lay down. I heard Leo arrive at the car later. It was dark. He called to me through the tent, "Laura, are you awake?"

"Yeah I am."

"I gotta invite to sleep at an Amish house, do you wanna come?"

"No, I'm in my sleeping bag," I said.

"You'll never get the chance again. Are you sure? I'll wait 'til you get dressed."

"Will we get a room together?" I asked.

"I dunno. You come if you want. I'm going anyhow."

"OK. I'm a-comin." I redressed, put the important things into my rucksack and got in the car. "I wasn't expecting this," I said. "I look a mess now."

"I wasn't expecting it either. Why don't you put your hair up?"

"Good thinking." He started the car as I found a hair clasp and started to knot it up. I'd still look like a crazy, sleepy traveller. Damn middle aged hair.

"I met a student called Ralph who's living with the Amish. I met the man of the family and the guy invited me to sleep at his house. The farm's at the edge of town. I said I gotta travel companion and he invited you too. His name's John Miller."

"It's very generous of him but aren't we too late?" I asked.

"No, I just left Ralph and he'll wait for us there. I think most of the family will be in bed but there's an outhouse building for guests that we can have. Ralph says John Miller likes to show non-Amish how they live and cos I'm from Europe ... it's too good to miss," he said.

We drove back to the centre of Topeka and out west of town. There were fireworks displays all over the place–tomorrow was 4 July.

Ralph was waiting outside the main farmhouse as we arrived and showed us to the guest building and so it was that I found myself within the space of an hour sharing an Amish double bed with Leo. That mattress was hard. It was the first time we'd shared a double bed.

"I don't think you're going to turn me down somehow," I said as I reached for him. He laughed shaking his head, "You're hot!"

"So are you sweetie. God these quilts, they're so heavy. I wonder what kind of sex those Amish have?" I said.

"Same kind as the rest of us," said Leo as he climbed on top of me. "Oh I forgot to tell you, I picked up a hitchhiker for the day we leave. He's a farmer from Uruguay." He may have been a lot of things Leo, but one thing he wasn't was racist. It felt good that night, the first time to be sleeping in the same bed.

In the morning I met John Miller and his wife Hannah who prepared an Amish cheese casserole and coffee for breakfast. I let Leo do the talking. They were discussing horses and farming equipment so I took the time to be quiet and submissive for once not like I had been in bed the night before. I was having memory flashes and as aroused as I'd ever been. The food was excellent and I wouldn't need anything more until evening.

After another day with farming equipment, we met up with Pablo, our Uruguay hitch-hiker. He hadn't gotten off his farm in seven years. He was tall and dark and sported a moustache with a twist at each end. He had no car and was having difficulty getting around the States without one. He spoke good English and offered me a beer. Some Amish came by in a little motorised farm car and asked us how long we were staying and where we were from. We said we would be gone by early morning.

50

Independence Day and three motley travellers—one French, one Uruguay, one Scot; one sommelier, one farmer, one writer—were riding the Rust Bucket from Topeka, Indiana headed out west on the W-700.

  I switched on the radio. The man said it was the seventy-fifth day of the oil spill. Our Uruguay friend fell asleep in the back and we remained quiet whilst watching the passing landscape. It was flat.

  At ten o'clock, we stopped for breakfast at a service station and whilst Leo and Pablo sat outside eating sandwiches, I bought some fresh bread and went back to the car. I had a jar of peanut butter stored in the trunk so I opened up the car and dug around for the box of food and a knife. I was sitting with the trunk open, peanut butter and bread in hand, when Leo came back. "You've messed up the trunk. I had it packed the way I wanted it. Now I'll have to do it again," he said.

  "Sorry," I said and I moved out of his way. I sat eating in the passenger seat with the door open whilst he re-arranged things in the back. Pablo decided to put his rucksack in there too. Suitably rearranged, we drove off.

  Later, we took a right turn in the direction of Goshen then onto the I-90 headed for Chicago. I wondered why we were going so far north when our journey was westwards but I kept this question to myself. We joined the I-94 and were driving towards the city when it dawned on me—we were going as far north as possible to meet the beginning of Route 66. I checked my guidebook–yes, it started in downtown Chicago. Leo wanted to traverse as much of it as possible.

Around one o'clock, we took a left turn onto the Stevenson Expressway and I-55 and thereafter found the exit–onto the old road, the frontage road, the mother road, the Will Rogers Highway, the mother of all roads, the most exciting road in the world according to some, and Leo's childhood ambition now come true–here we were and I was about to get another kick, this time on Route 66.

"So here we are and this is it!" I said. "Happy?" I looked at Leo.

"Yeah, I've wanted to do this all my life," he said. The pressure was lifting. We slowed now, we were on a two lane highway. It ran alongside the freeway. We followed the brown and white road signs 'HISTORIC ROUTE ILLINOIS US 66' through some two-bit towns. The tarmac was a bit of a trundle at times and old style American graphics and signs began to make their appearance.

51

Beyond Normal, we stopped next at Dixie Truckers Home in McLean. The guidebook said it was a funky Route 66 diner that never closed except for a fire one day in 1965. Sadly, and unbelievably, it was closed today of all days, Sunday 4 July–under new management. Nobody was home except the builders so we walked across the tarmac to a McDonald's where Leo ordered a Big Mac and a burger chaser. Pablo, a Quarter Pounder with Cheese. I had fries.

"What's with the burger chaser? Isn't a Big Mac enough?" I asked Leo as we sat down.

"I'm hungry," he said and took a bite.

"What do they call a Big Mac in France?" asked Pablo.

"*C'est Le Big Mac.*"

"This one is a *McNifica* in Uruguay," said Pablo, pointing at his burger.

"And you have *McNifica* whiskers," I said.

"That's a *Royale Deluxe* in France," said Leo.

I never ate a hamburger in America. I could eat just one proper meal a day on this car trip or else I'd end up looking like one. Veni, vidi, veggie. I came, I saw, I had a veggie burger. If I wanted to experience the All That Is, then I'd got to eat decent food. *Malbouffe* made you fat and stupid. Food processing destroyed enzymes, including the ones that precurse DMT, what some call the spirit molecule. It came from the pineal gland. That's if I had any pineal gland left after being microwaved by wifi in New York.

Back in the car and a stop at Atlanta for Bunyon's Statue–a fiberglass giant holding a hotdog. We drove along through Lincoln, Elkhart, Williamsville. There was no end to spotting old murals, signs and advertising. At Springfield when the old road ended for a time, we had to drive across the city. Leo was keen to offload Pablo now but the train station was deserted. It was 4th July, after all. There was no up-to-date timetable either. At a Subway for a coffee and wifi, the plan was hatched to take our friend to the Greyhound bus station back at the edge of town. I didn't see why Pablo couldn't stay with us–he could keep the peace and pay for some of the gas after all.

An abandoned car and a boy from Texas were outside the closed bus station later. He said he had lost his job and was returning home. Our car was going on to St Louis and we could quite easily have taken them both with us but Leo didn't let on. We said our goodbye to Pablo. The two of us were on our own once more, any tension covered up by the radio. We were driving back again through Springfield.

"Do you know what that music is?" I asked Leo. "It's kinda awful."

"I dunno, it sounds classical," he said.

"It's an orchestra playing Abba, *Thank You For The Music*. I wish these classical musos would stay away from pop. They murder it."

By around three thirty, we reunited with the 66 at the other side of Springfield. There had always been a risk of a wrong turning but we got there in the end with the help of my guidebook. I decided to broach conversation. "Did you ever read a book that changed your life?" I asked Leo.

"Yeah, Satish Kumar, the one where he goes on a pilgrimage for world peace."

"Yeah, like that worked ... I saw him talking once."

"You did?"

"Yeah, he gives a lot of talks, he's a big greenie," I said. "He called Oxford and Cambridge centres of ignorance. I'd never heard such a thing. It blew my mind then I realised he was right." I shook my head. "He said the western political mantra was 'economic growth, economic growth, economic growth'."

"I think my mantra's better." I laughed out loud.

"Have you ever walked the Santiago trail? That's a pilgrimage walk and it starts in France."

"No but I reckon my three years travelling was a pilgrimage in a way."

"I thought a pilgrimage was for a spiritual purpose."

"Wine–that's a spiritual purpose." He smacked his right hand against the wheel. "I travelled for farming. I travelled overland all through Russia, the middle east and in India, working on vineyards and tea and coffee plantations, farming, everything." He loosened and regripped the wheel with both hands. "Then I took an overland trip back doing the same. Now that was a pilgrimage."

"That was a quest." I paused. "Did you ever read any American writers?"

"God, you ask a lot of questions."

"I thought we could get to know each other better. Why don't you ask me something instead?" I said.

"OK. Did you ever read any American writers?"

"That was my question. God you're annoying," I sighed. "Yeah loads of them. Hemingway, Scott Fitzgerald, Carrie Bradshaw–oh, I forgot she's not real."

"We read Hemingway at school, *A Moveable Feast*–it's all about Paris. He liked to travel didn't he?"

"Yeah, just like you. He shot himself in the head in the end. He was so macho but he was married all his life. He couldn't be alone. We're way tougher than he ever was, going at things alone. I read another Hemingway–the one about bullfighting, *Death In The Afternoon*. Did you ever read any Scottish writers?"

"I don't think so, I've never heard of any."

"I bet you've heard of *Trainspotting*. That was Irvine Welsh. But Robert Burns is the famous one. A twist from one of his poems inspired the title to *Catcher In The Rye*."

"You read that book?" Leo looked at me.

"Actually I have."

"Did you like it?"

"It goes on a bit. The guy is in the middle of a breakdown. His brother has died and he's flunking out of school." I paused for a moment. "Do you think we're flunking out?" I asked.

"You might be, I'm not."

"Have you read *The Grapes of Wrath*? It's all about farming."

"No. Wasn't it a film? I don't remember, tell me about it," he said.

"It's about the Oklahoma dust bowl. Years of bad farming, then drought and then wind blew the topsoil away so farmers defaulted on their loans because they couldn't grow anything. The banks foreclosed so everyone drove west to California on Route 66 looking for work. The book's about the Joad family and their drive to California. Lots of Okies died on that trip. Steinbeck called the 66 The Mother Road, the first road of America but it was really cobbled from the roads that were already there."

"You know a lot about stuff," said Leo.

"I read the guidebook, that's all. Besides I'm not a wine guy."

"What do you mean by that?"

"I'm not specialised in anything, that's all. I know a little bit about lots of things."

"Maybe you don't know French culture."

"Maybe not–try me."

"OK. So who wrote *The Hunchback of Notre Dame*?"

"Victor Hugo. But I haven't read it–have you?"

"Yeah at school."

"Is it a good read?"

"I preferred *Les Miserables*."

"I haven't read that either. It's set in the revolution, no? The French Revolution was the birth of the modern world, wasn't it? The birth of the individual and the Romantics–I think that's where you and me come in."

"I'm a winemaker, a farmer. *Un paysan*. I don't know about anything else."

"That's romantic. I'd love to be a *paysanne*, a peasant, I hate the modern world sometimes."

"I'm gonna make wine. Cheese too–a small mixed *petit domaine*."

"You're a big cheese in a small car, the real McCoy."

He was a big cheese, but it was my feet that were stinking. I got out the deodorant again and rolled it over my feet, crossing my leg and hanging one foot at a time to dry.

"What does that mean?"

"It's an expression. It's like Coke, The Real Thing. It was about Scots whisky at the time."

"You like to talk a lot."

"I never seem to get to know you though."

"I like wine, I like travel, I like exploring. It's all you need to know."

52

We approached St Louis now, across the Mississippi of Mark Twain (in my mind anyhow) on another of those American bridges from *Cheers* and stopped at the other side. We had crossed the county line into Missouri. Time to visit the tourist office before it closed. It was a ritual.

We were advised to take the freeway and I cussed out that office later because they directed us onto the city circular. They seemed to think the city was dangerous. I mean, *really*. Leo had never heard of *Meet Me In St Louis* and said we hadn't time to go back. We didn't realise quite how circular the route was until we were on it and couldn't find a way off.

The tourist office got one thing right. They said, pay a visit to Ted Drewes for the frozen custard. Back to Chippewa Street to stand in line for a Tart Cherry and Praline Custard. Leo ate the Cardinal Sin Sundae. It was the best ever. I bought a coffee after and we drove off once more.

We struggled to get back onto the 66 which was my fault, of course. I was the one with the guidebook. We had gained in miles from the freeway but found ourselves driving around and around trying to find a place to stop for the night. Leo was increasingly frustrated to find somewhere. You could set a clock by it. Campsites for recreational vehicles proved too expensive and Leo was now getting MAD. I noticed a Kampgrounds Of America site nearby from a leaflet I'd picked up along the line and offered to pay for the night. It was cheap. At dusk–a pattern for us for stopping–we found the campsite and parked outside the office. It still had a light on. We entered and I noticed a sign: 'Primitive Tent $20' and I guessed that was me.

Primitive tent duly pitched, I had a swim in the pool even though it was nearly dark. I hadn't had a shower for seven days. The sky dulled darker with night and clouds and then rain came with thunder. I fled to the tent just in time. Primitive or not, it would keep me warm and dry. Ten minutes passed whilst I settled into my sleeping bag, and then I heard Leo's voice.

"Laura, have you got my sleeping bag?"

"No," I said. I was worried.

"I can't find it. It's not in the trunk. I don't know where it is," he said.

I lay there for a couple of minutes and switched on my torch and looked around the tent. It was ridiculous. Of course I didn't have his sleeping bag in there with me.

I got dressed and crawled out into the rain and the dark and opened the car door and sat in the passenger seat. Leo was seated in the back.

"Where did you last have it?" I asked. I felt guilty, like it was my fault. I knew he blamed me for everything that went wrong and looked for every reason to give me a hard time.

"I had it this morning when I packed it in the car," he said.

"Do you think Pablo could have taken it?" I asked.

"I can't believe he would, after we helped him. I don't want to think that," he said.

"I remember taking stuff out of the car at lunchtime when we stopped for food," I said.

"I don't remember seeing my sleeping bag and I put everything back afterwards. Surely I didn't leave something lying on the pavement?"

"I don't remember if it was even on the back seat of the car. We had extra stuff on board with Pablo. I can't believe he would have done that. I don't want to believe it," he said. I knew he was directing the problem at me.

"Let's have a look again in the trunk," I said. We got out in the dark and in the drizzle with Leo wearing a lamp around his head and we opened the trunk. I was terrified in case it was my fault–I would never hear the end of it.

I put my hand in and pulled aside a holdall. Something slipped between two boxes. I put my hand down in between the two boxes and pulled out–a black sleeping bag! Scrunched up in its scruncher but it was there nonetheless. I was saved!

"Here it is!" I held up the bag and he took it from me. "Now, can you just be in a good mood for once today?" I demanded. "I deserve a kiss for putting up with all this." I reached forward and planted a kiss on his mouth. He smiled. He stepped back and opened the backdoor of the car and I followed him inside. Everyone on the campsite was inside their RVs and we were inside the RB. Having sex. It was 10 pm maybe. No-one would have seen the rocking of the car.

"I'm done," he said later as he had done before when he had had enough and left things sky high. "OK," I said. I was used to it by now and I let him have his moment. He wasn't worth challenging. It wasn't worth being upset. This is the deal, take it or leave it.

I left it, and the car and went back to my sleeping bag and my primitive tent and fell asleep.

53

I awoke happy the following morning. It was sunny with a light breeze. Leo was swimming in the pool so I joined him. He was absorbed in himself floating around. I was trying to gauge his mood like a slave to a master or a child to a parent. A critical parent at that.

He brought me a coffee as I packed up my stuff later. He was in a very good mood. He blogged for ages and then showered and began a cook up. We should have left by midday but no-one seemed to mind, we weren't taking up a lot of space. I even managed to wash and dry some clothes in the sunshine and we ate rice and vegetables–Leo with ketchup, mine without.

We set off for the Mother Road at around 2 pm. Leo took a turquoise paisley scarf out of his bag and tied it around his head whilst he began to drive. He completed his look with rose-tinted sunglasses.

"You look completely nuts," I said.

"We're on the road now," he replied. *"C'est le rock 'n' roll!"*

The next couple of days were a blur for me on the 66. Looking back, I realise it was because we didn't have any fights. I remember crossing Big Piney River at Devil's Elbow, stopping at Wrink's Market in Lebanon and buying bottles of Route 66 coca cola and giving my empty bottle to Leo. I had no space for carrying souvenirs.

I remember getting lost a few times–the road would disappear on us as we took older sections that hadn't been maintained. On a rainy morning, I remember a diner full of old men where I ate biscuits and gravy for the first time. I remember stopping for photos at the biggest chair in the world and the old Phillips serving station at Cuba. I remember we parked up for the night in a dead stretch of the old road that ended up in weeds. I had real trouble pitching my tent as the sun went down and a police car drove close by. We slept well but got up extra early, a feeling all of its own to be up with the orange sun in anticipation of our first coffee stop.

There weren't many cars on the 66, sometimes fancy 1950s cars, sometimes groups of riders on Harleys. We were surrounded by cornfields as we drove through the dozen miles of the old road that was Kansas and left Kansas again giving me the opportunity to say: "Leo, I've a feeling we're not in Kansas anymore" but it was lost on him. He'd never seen *The Wizard of Oz*.

I even got the netbook out and typed up for Leo's blog as we drove along, him dictating to me, but by and large there was no time for writing and blogging as we were headed west for his appointment with the wine consultant.

It was then that we started experimenting with masturbating in the car. I don't know why I did it, it's not as if I needed his approval. I reached over with my left hand whilst he was at the wheel and took it out. He said he found it relaxing. I didn't, it was a bit of a strain and I got bored with it.

54

When we got into Oklahoma, he said to me, "Tell me more about *The Grapes Of Wrath*. You know the dust bowl and all that."

"They farmed wrong, they didn't look after their topsoil. Just like now, really. I mean, look at all that corn out there. There's nothing else in sight. Our bodies are made from food, right? What if all the *malbouffe* is made from corn? That's what you're looking at out there, that's what all that corn is for, for high fructose corn syrup and it's made from oil not soil. Oil-produced corn syrup. If you eat *malbouffe*, that is, and nearly everything has *malbouffe* now." We were looking at the Green Revolution gone bad. What good were revolutions anyhow? The bible said the meek would inherit the earth but I was still waiting. A truly post industrial society? Now that would be revolutionary.

"Yeah and we go to war to get the oil to grow the food that depletes the soil and makes us fat and sick so we die early," said Leo. It was depressing. "This culture wants you sick to get you consuming, it's got no interest in balance and health. It's topsoil we need to be creating more of, more than anything else. They gotta hold of the food production, once they gotta hold of the water, we're finished. It's a war on *terroir*."

"So it's like, dude, where's my topsoil?"

"Yeah, it's topsoil we should be growing. There'd have been no dust bowl if they'd farmed biodynamically," he said "and if we listened to our hearts, we wouldn't get heart disease."

"Kill people off with junk food–it's a hell of a lot easier than waging warfare. Too fat to fight."

"Too fat to fuck, so the population gets reduced anyhow. The first agrochemicals were made from post-war weapons stockpiles, did you know that? It's a war on *terroir* from first to last."

"Do you think biodynamics can change things?"

"It's making a difference in wine and I'm gonna find some in California."

"Can you really make a wine with emotion?"

"Sure you can. Those mass produced wines, they've eliminated the inner life of the wine, the vine. They've turned wine into an object, something to be consumed."

"It's like we're killing the living daylights out of everything."

"And so a living wine will generate feeling inside you, instead of being dead you become alive to the nuance of life."

"Ooo! I like the sound of that!"

"When you have people who can feel life on the inside, you can't control them. Objective reality is a con, I found that out in India. Everything we see, everything we experience is internal. Everything. We experience everything internally."

Was it really that simple? Objective-subjective, major-minor, did a subtler nuance prevail? If we drew back the curtain of science, would we find songlines crossed the earth?

"I didn't know you were so high-minded, I'm impressed. I expect natural wines will find a niche market."

"A niche market suits me fine."

"OK, so what would you do if you were in charge? What would you do if you were *Il Presidente*?"

"I'm not Spanish."

"OK, The President. President of the Fifth Republic of France."

"I'd marry a supermodel."

"That's been done. She's a musician by the way. Just thought I'd mention it. OK, so you'd marry a supermodel. What else would you do?"

"I don't want to be *Il Presidente*."

"I thought you weren't Spanish."

"I'd have wine pouring out of the taps instead of into the European wine lake. I'd make everybody study biodynamics. I'd hate to be president of France."

"Yeah, me too. I'd hate to be married to one. There's never been a woman president yet?"

"No."

"Politics is horrible. I'm amazed that even men want to do it."

"I just wanna have my farm–president of my own little republic."

"And find a supermodel to farm it with. She could wear Chanel. She could start a Chanel farmwear line for women farmers. Hey did you know that women make up most of the farmers of the world?"

"Yeah, I've been to India, remember?"

"I bet it's still men that own the land they farm though. I just hate men sometimes."

"Don't think too much. It's the intellect that causes the trouble. Just be physical."

55

We arrived in Amarillo on a rainy Wednesday morning. Texas was flat and not like I imagined at all.

After eggs, hash browns and coffee in a diner, the next thing I knew we were in a car mechanics to change the other two tyres. It took up most of the afternoon. Leo said, "It's gonna cost you $120." He didn't ask, he demanded the money from me. When he saw my expression, he said, "Well you know what you can do if you don't like it."

"It's not as if I'm driving all the way through California and into Canada like you are," I protested but I handed over the money.

"Maybe I'll ask you to pay some towards the car insurance as well." The thought occurred to me to write a feminist tract on how to handle the man in your life. I'd call it 'His Mother, HimSelf'. Well, someone needs to.

We drove on with new tyres later that afternoon and stopped at a McDonald's to eat and use the internet. I had lost tent pegs somewhere along the way and asked Leo if we could go to buy new ones as it was raining heavily outside. He dismissed me. "I'm organising my thirtieth birthday party back in France later in the year. I'm busy."

Thanks. I'm about to pitch up in the rain without decent pegs and you're organising a party in four months' time. I was hanging around waiting for him and had respect when he was researching and writing his blog but I had noticed once before, sometimes he was on Facebook and it annoyed me. Why couldn't he be with me? Weren't we travelling together? Was I just a money supply? Worse, was I a sex supply? I couldn't possibly bring this up in any way for fear of causing an argument but it didn't help the underlying tension. He was a selfish oaf.

He suggested I find out where the nearest Walmart's was and he would collect me later. But would he find me? And how would I call him? He looked at his phone once a day. He gave up his party planning in a hot fury and we drove out to the other edge of town to a WalMart. I bought heavy duty tent pegs as it was all I could find. I walked up to the fast food place he was using to get back online again and gave up on him. I crossed the road to another store and bought a beer and sat in the car drinking it.

It was late, still raining and getting dark. We were back on the freeway heading west and Leo was fuming. It was my fault we hadn't found a place for the night. We took a turning off the freeway and there was a side road and he said, "You want us to take this road? Do you? DO YOU?" I thought he wanted me to say yes so I said so, not wanting to feed his mood. We turned onto this dirt road and drove further and further and he shouted, "This is the road you wanted! This is what you wanted! Are you happy now?" He braked the car suddenly. He tried to start it again and we couldn't move. I heard the Rust Bucket's new fancy tyres whirr as the engine groaned and we sank into mud. "That's it, we're stuck," said Leo. "We gonna have to spend the night here and get out of this in the morning." I pitched my tent with the new heavy duty pegs in thick mud, in darkness, next to the car. In the distance, I could see the freeway. In the other direction, an intermittent red light. I got in.

I thought there'd be a payoff. I thought God would have kept her side of the bargain. I thought by now I would have found love and refuge. All I'd found was an abusive man. A need for redemption was driving me. Would I make it? To give up everything and walk this tightrope–for nothing? When I found there was nothing, would I gain the world? Wasn't that another bargain? I seemed to have been living with a hundred invisible premises, one of which came back and back–bargaining with God.

Bargaining with God was what people did when they were told they were dying, but I was too young still, and too much of a coward for that. I believed if I followed my path, that there would be a payoff. Where was the bloody payoff? There was always wine, of course. And The X Factor and the movies were a nice kind of safe haven–you'd only have to face up to things when your dog died. Wasn't there a more meaningful existence? There had to be another pact, another way.

    I didn't believe in a universe with no meaning, the meaning would be the one I gave it. There were infinite layers to reality and if I focussed on one meaning then that would be true, if I focussed on another, then that would be true too. I seemed to have been programmed from birth or earlier by something else–an absence of something. Of what? Some structure in my sad psyche was missing. I had been swimming in a sea of consciousness without a lifeboat. I had had analysis but it no longer held true. I had to make my own divine cut, my own diamond sutra. This planet was my home. Mother Earth, Father Sky–I was a wave on the ocean and could enjoy the ride.

56

I heard the car door click in the morning, it was ten to seven. I opened up the tent and saw Leo in no mood for what was in front of us. The front wheels, maybe the back wheels were stuck in mud. I heard the distant sound of cars on the freeway and saw an abandoned house to our right and behind us, a quarter of a mile away, another farmhouse with no lights on and a tractor on its front road. The flashing blue light in the distance turned out to be an airfield in the light of the new Texas morning. I dressed and packed up the muddy tent.

Leo wore flip flops at first and started to gather straw to put under our new tyres. "We need straw and stones to put under the wheels," he bellowed. I followed suit, walking on eggshells and mud. My boots were a mess. Leo took off his flip flops and worked in his bare feet, his beige, cotton-pickin' hemp pants rolled up to his knees. He was cussing me in French. We made repeated trips with stones and straw and lay them behind all four wheels. Leo got in the car and revved it up in reverse as I pushed. It was useless. I had no upper arm strength.

"We came down this side road because you wanted it," shouted Leo. We revved and pushed once more. I could only pretend to have strength. What little I had was lost with my feet slipping back on the mud. We gathered more stones and straw with repeated treks over the mud to find them and lay them down under the tyres.

I said nothing that morning. I retained absolute silence while Leo dumped every last piece of verbal abuse until, on a sixth attempt, the car moved. It had taken the best part of an hour. My boots were something to behold and Leo had mud up to his lovely French knees.

I placed my boots in a plastic bag and wore sandals in the car. Leo wiped his feet with a towel and drove barefoot. I found it rather sexy. There was something wrong with the Rust Bucket and I was to pay to fix it, he said. We continued our journey. Luckily whatever was wrong with the Rust Bucket magically fixed itself whilst we were in motion and I switched on Route 66 Radio to find The Beatles *'We Can Work It Out'* as at last the sun came out and we were back on the two lane highway again, running parallel to the freeway. Less than an hour later we arrived at Adrian and stopped for The MidPoint Cafe. We were officially halfway to L A from Chicago, 1,139 miles in each direction. It was due to be a hot day. I took out my boots now baked dry in Texas mud. I drew commiserating glances from fellow drivers and bikers who clearly had been nowhere near the rain as I sliced mud off my boots with my penknife.

The cafe was built originally in the 1930s and was fabulously awash with souvenirs and fifties retro. I would have offered to pay for breakfast, yet I realised it would make no difference to Leo's mood. I sat at a window table on my own and drank the first coffee of the day, taking in the surroundings. I felt like a human being again. "They've got your guidebook," he called over from the other side of the room as I stared at the big '66' on the wall. There was 66 paraphernalia everywhere. The cafe had lifted his mood and we ate a full breakfast of eggs, bacon, sausages, toast, hash browns together. We needed it.

Outside in a yard sale I bought a Route 66 t-shirt with a map on the back for $1. I took a photo of Leo by the big tourist sign outside before continuing the journey.

We gained an hour at the New Mexico border. It was now 9am. I said to Leo, "I just want to say one thing to you–Taos. I'd like to place the thought in your mind. The first ever Earthship was built there, you know." An Earthship is a house built of used tyres and I knew he was fascinated by them.

"We haven't got the time to go to the Grand Canyon and Taos." His mood had turned darker again. "And I wanna see the Canyon."

The tourist office was light and airy with lots of maps and guides. I poured myself a free coffee. Leo asked about Taos. There was a pow-wow open to the public that evening. It would be a four hour drive. As we got back into the car, Leo said, "OK. We're going." I could never know what was in his mind, or how it worked.

"Thank you for changing your mind," I said.

"I'm not doing it for you," came his reply.

57

Just because I was *pronoid*, did it mean the Universe was out to help me? If I made a wish, did it really come true?

When I'd made a decision to go on the road, when I'd been writing out the gratitude journal, I hadn't been intending or wishing to visit Taos. That thought had never occurred to me. I scoured my mind. The experience had no meaning or value outside of the one I was having. The Universe wasn't out there, responding to requests. It was in me. It was me. I was in it. A part of my consciousness and the energy that creates worlds was entangled in a quantum mystery. If I had a thought or a wish, it was happening in that quantum field too. If I fully believed in it, what I wanted might come quicker. My negativity and resistance could get in the way. My lack of faith would manifest in a lack of result–how could it not? Negativity would operate in the quantum field too.

Just because I was pronoid, did it mean the Universe was out to help me? The answer came like the answer to a Zen koan–resolutely, YES. There was no other way. I wasn't alone in the universe, I was dancing to a divine rhythm inside a bohemian rhapsody.

To Albuquerque through the Sandia Mountains, approaching the city from the east. We made a lunch stop before taking the road north and ate *huevos rancheros*–refried beans with fried eggs and lots of cheese, plenty of chilli. Leo said to me: "How come you know about New Mexico?"

"All my favourite writers have lived here. I read about it in their books."

North from Albuquerque on the Pan American Freeway now until we reached a small town called Las Vegas and took a turn onto highway 518. Higher into the mountains, into extravagant land, a wild country which was exactly the song that was on the radio, *Wild Country*. Wake Owl–I'd never heard of the band before. The lyrics needed bringing home a little more, but the voice! I wound down the window fully and just at that moment, Leo turned the radio off. I sometimes wondered whether silence was the opposite of music, music the opposite of silence. There was something to be said for breathing nature, listening to its fragrance, tasting its vision. God was a master craftsman, none of it flawed so neither was I, neither was Leo. It's just that so often it didn't seem that way.

"Wow, this is just like Nepal," said Leo, breaking the silence. He stopped the car and we walked out to drink the Sangre de Cristo mountains, the silence deepening without the RB engine, a symphony of silence. "I think I prefer nature to culture," said Leo.

"I think I do too. Today, anyway."

We arrived at Taos in the rush hour–it had all the usual modern American roads and businesses surrounding it. Out of town and onto the reservation, we paid $5 each for a day pass and pitched beneath the Sacred Mountain for the 25th annual Taos Pueblo Pow Wow.

There was a good feel in the air, an air of anticipation. I left Leo alone and wandered as stalls were being pitched, cars arrived, people appeared in costume and feathers, beads and buckskin, multi-coloured ribbons trailing, blankets, ponchos, shawls, fringes. Tepees pierced the skyline. I listened to a herbalist as she explained how to burn sage to cleanse a new home.

We separated for most of the evening. I was free. Free for fast food and *empanadita* and *chimichanga* as they slipped off my tongue at a food stall, then into my mouth. Free to watch the show in the central arena. Better still, to listen to the drummers around the arena fringes, singing in groups of mainly men, sometimes women, of up to twenty. I was enthral to the drumming.

That night, on the roof of the earth, beneath the Sacred Mountain, in my primitive tent, the drumming soothed me into a deep sleep. I dreamt I was walking on the seabed with my mother and grandmother. A wooden chest that lay there broke open and silvery doves like fish, flew out from the bottom of the sea into the blue sky.

I said hello to a few people here and there in the morning and gazed up at that Sacred Mountain. I found myself in a conversation with someone climbing out of their van from sleep. Taos was twinned with Nepal in the earth etheric, she said, and human bullshit can't function at 7,000 feet above sea level–it's why Taos was for spiritual seekers. I looked around and there was Leo riding a Mustang bareback, and bare-chested. He was grinning from ear to ear.

"You look very happy this morning," I said. "Where'd you find the horse?"

"I just had breakfast tacos with a native guy. He's a horse dealer."

"You look great."

"I stayed up late with the drummers 'round a fire, smoking. I swear when I was walking back to the car I could feel the heartbeat of the earth through my feet."

"You're nuts."

"No, it was the Schumann Resonance!"

"What's the Schumann Resonance?"

"It's the electromagnetic field of the earth, the heartbeat."

"And it's named after a composer? I love it."

"No, Schumann was a scientist. He discovered it."

"And he named it after a composer? I love it. That was one cool scientist." The planet was a divine expression of femininity but still its heart had a man's name. At least he was a musician–to me anyway.

We drove out over the Rio Grande high up on the Gorge Bridge late morning, passing jewellery and food stalls to take a look at the Earthship. It looked like a spaceship up here on the mesa. There was a community of them, all dug into the landscape with their sloping glass solar fronts, their construction of rubber tyres and glass bottles left visible in the architecture. "It feels like being on the moon up here," said Leo.

"Apparently the guy who created these got the idea when he was meditating under a pyramid," I said.

We wandered around the visitor centre in amazement. They were growing bananas inside beneath the windows.

Back in town, we made a wholefoods stop where I bought piñon coffee and ground it in the store. I prepared bagels with cheddar for us on the roof of the car before we began our journey once more.

Driving south through the mountains and the scenery, happy again. Onto the freeway this time as we were headed back south to meet the 66 and a visit tomorrow to the north part of the Grand Canyon. The sun was beginning to set as we slipped into Arizona, stopping for gas and two tins of beer.

58

Heavy rain came and at dusk we stopped the car in front of another KOA office and ran in. There was no way my primitive tent could be pitched on a bunch of Arizona stones in the rain and in the dark so I paid for a hut for the night. "Good thinking, buddy," said Leo.

The little hut wasn't perfect what with the plastic cover on the beds but we made it cosy with light and Ravi Shankar playing on Leo's netbook. By 10pm, we were eating snacks and drinking our tins of beer. It was a peace of sorts to have a room for the night but still I felt like a fugitive.

"Have you finished your beer yet?" Leo asked.

"I have now," I said, taking a last drink and placing the empty can on the floor. He came over to my bed and opened and spread around our two sleeping bags on the mattress and took off his t-shirt. I said nothing, listening to the rain on the roof of the hut. The image I have of that night is of a naked and magnificent Leo with either leg astride me wearing nothing but a necklace of Nepal beads.

He penetrated me to the delicate twang of the sitar and the pelting of rain on the roof. I would forever associate Ravi Shankar with the hottest sex of my life. So exhausted later, I was the one to fall asleep afterwards.

I could have slept for hours the following morning, despite the noise of the freeway. Leo came over to my bed once more. He obviously wanted his money's worth although I had been the one to pay for the night.

I said to him afterwards, "You were amazing last night. It's your personality that doesn't quite match up."

"It's your perception that's the problem," he said. We left around midday, later than we ought and I was quite literally knackered.

59

Away from the 66 again, through the desert all afternoon towards the North Canyon, arriving in early evening. It was cooling now and there were still lots of people around. It was magnificent of course but somehow I wasn't moved by it. I couldn't understand my lack of emotion. I was nothing if not emotional. I didn't really get the point of staring at it though I'd stared at many a thing in my life. It seemed too big to be comprehended. Seeing those fireflies had broken me open, that little red bird in the tree had moved me more.

Leo talked with a ranger and was told of a good spot in the national park where we could camp for free and have a view of the canyon for sunrise so we went driving in search of it. We drove for nearly two hours, lastly through a close pine forest in the dark then gave up on finding the beauty spot and stopped along the road where there was a clearing and I pitched my tent there.

As I took my things from the car, Leo said to me through the narrow opening in the window, "Goodnight Laura." I didn't reply. I was scared and I wanted him to take care of me. There were bears out there. "Goodnight Laura," he said again. I still didn't reply. "Are you OK?" he said.

"No, I'm scared."

"What is there to be scared of?"

"It's dark and we're in the middle of a forest and I'm scared. Good night."

I got into my tent and switched on my little radio for company until I fell asleep.

The pine-filled fragrant pollution-free air didn't stop Leo complaining in the morning that I never did any cooking and I said, "It's your Nepal cooking stove. You'd go crazy if I damaged it and I don't know how to use it."

He showed me how to light and gauge the flame of the stove and I boiled a pan of water for piñon coffee. I spooned two heaped tablespoons into the hot water and stirred, replacing it onto the heat and taking it off a couple of times to percolate.

"Wow, that aroma is like chocolate," said Leo.

"It's piñon coffee, I bought it at the store yesterday, it's got Mexican pine nuts in," I said. It was the best coffee I ever tasted.

Some hours later we were back on the 66 in Arizona and stopped in Kingman for a break at Mr D's Diner. It was a terrific place, another fabulous fifties diner, and it had to be *huevos rancheros* once more and when the food arrived, the tortilla chips were red, yellow and blue. Leo called his brother in France for the entirety of the meal. He also spoke to the biodynamic consultant in California and made a date to meet and work with him in L A. Leo and I would be parting company the day before and he would drop me off at Union Station. I'd decided to take a train up to San Francisco to spend a few days there.

We turned onto the freeway again to catch up on time. "I love those American diners," said Leo. "That's the best one we've been in so far."

"I agree, it's just that I don't like the fifties," I said. "And I don't get all that American fifties high school stuff either. I just don't like it."

"My brother was asking about you on the phone," said Leo. "I told him you were very adventurous."

"I suppose that's flattering."

"How come you never talk about your family?"

"Sometimes I do. I was in France at my sister's before I came to America," I explained. "I'm a walking political statement to them. They've got no concept of freedom and reaching for it, they've never taken a risk in their lives. All I am to them is a woman who can't get a man. It's like their minds are stuck in the fifties. It's probably why I don't like those fifties diners much. They pretend to like me but really they'd rather I didn't exist, I disturb them so much, so metaphorically they try to destroy me."

"I think you're reading too much into it Laura."

"I think I'm not reading enough into it. Maybe that's the difference between you and me. It's between freedom and conformity."

"I'm not a conformist," he said.

"Did you ever read *The Philosophy of Freedom?* The whole point of the the human being is freedom. Freedom's the thing you know."

"You still gotta work. You can't escape forever."

"How do you know? What do you mean by escape? You're just repeating what you've heard elsewhere."

"You need to work."

"You believe you need to work. What you need is a degree of cash to survive–you don't need to work always and forever." He was still captive to the machine. Maybe it suited him. It had never suited me, I was born to be wild.

"If you live to work, then you are a machine. You're captive, that's what machines do–they work. They function. Human beings by nature are nomads, wanderers. I thought you were one. I should have realised when you loved those fifties diners–they represent a horror story. Captive, domestic, clean, polished, nicey nicey. I'm not stupid. People hate my freedom, lots of people do. One day they'll hate yours too but it's easier for you because you're a man. Look, I'm not saying it's easy, I'm saying it's hard. It's bad enough throwing off the shackles of a lifetime without other people and their stupid opinions. Women barely worked a generation ago and now I'm supposed to have a male-styled career. I don't want one! And it's not about having a job or not having one. No-one need have a job anymore with the internet. It's a freedom to think. To think differently–it's the only freedom left. There's barely a link between work and wages now. If you're a banker and you screw the economy and the planet, you still get a bonus at Christmas, even if you're an atheist! All this claptrap about people having to get a job is plain hooey. There's plenty for everyone, in fact, there's too much stuff already. It's a monopoly of distribution that's the problem. There's no counter-culture, it's all been co-opted, it all gets co-opted and you can't stay ahead of the machine anymore.

What you can do is throw a few scraps to the hounds, keep them at bay and wander off to your heart's content."

"And you said it was me that was angry. Well, whilst we're here, Steiner said 'Only one who is morally unfree turns away from a fellow human being if the latter does not obey the same instincts and demands as himself.'"

"Only one who is morally unfree turns away from a fellow human being if the latter does not obey the same instincts and demands as himself," I repeated trying to understand what he had just said. "God, that guy was a bad writer. And I'm not angry." I paused. "Actually I am. I know my sisters aren't free–that's why they're dangerous. They're always trying to tell me what to do."

"My mother is always trying to tell me what to do."

"No-one likes being told what to do."

"Lots of people like it. That's why they're not on a mad road trip like us."

Perhaps my journey wasn't an escape after all, maybe I could think of it as a big kiss, a big embrace to reality. A step up into fear, into what was at the other side. After enlightenment–oh, I'll have another glass of wine.

We took one last stop at a fast food joint and the girl behind the counter told us her father had won $60,000 one night at a casino in Vegas. And so it was that I found myself in the early evening tailback on the Nevada border at the Hoover Dam. I was still eating French fries. "I had no idea we were coming to Vegas," I said, my mouth half-full, my fingers greasy.

"I'm only in the US once so I'm making the most of it," said Leo. "Are you happy you came?" Was I? I didn't feel happy, on the other hand, what else was there to do?

"I am when I see the scenery and the wildlife." All I could see at that moment was desert and cars. God, how I hated cars. "You know, last December I started using something called a gratitude journal. Every day for three months when I was drinking my morning coffee I wrote, 'I am so happy and grateful that Leo and I are spending our summer together' and I felt what it might be like."

"You're a witch!"

"It's the law of attraction. It was an experiment. It seems to have worked," I said. I omitted to tell him the full sentence, you know, the part about us being in love.

"But it was me that asked you to come, not the other way around," he said, stealing one of my fries.

"It was an inside job," I said. "Maybe everything is in the end, you know, all an inside job. It's all an illusion."

"When I was in India, I took ten days of silent meditation. All sorts of stuff came out of my mind. It *is* an illusion the reality out there but I thought you had to be a holy man to change it." The car moved forward an inch.

"I heard a politician on the TV once. He said the most interesting thing I ever heard a politician say."

"What was that?"

"It was after 9/11 and he said, 'It's like something out of a Hollywood movie. It's like we imagine it first and then it happens."

"The terrorists imagined it first."

"Hollywood imagined it too. It's like there's a group consciousness download. The writers and the scientists and the terrorists have the download at the same time but it manifests in different ways because their belief systems are different. Have you seen *The Matrix?* It says we're a projection from another reality."

"No, we're in a multidimensional reality, it's not separate. We all live in it and we all affect it. It's no wonder people get the same ideas at the same time. Especially if you're creative, you're always poking around in other realms. That old Hawaiian guy I met in India had it right. He called it the Superconscious."

"Tell me more."

"The trouble with the Superconscious is this though. It blocks where inspiration comes from, where everything comes from. He called that The Void. Everything comes from The Void."

"I went to an art gallery called The Void," I said.

"We're so busy in our little bubbles, we block it off. That's why you say 'I love you' to everything, to clear the shit, or the memories replaying, he called it."

"I love you," I said. He laughed.

"By saying 'I love you' to everything, the energy of everything, there's a hope you clear the noise so inspiration comes, you see?"

"I see." I relaxed a little into the seat, took a deep breath and said, "I love you."

"So now you have a mantra too."

"This stuff's easy."

"Then try saying it to your sisters." I stuffed the last French fries into my mouth.

"What you gonna manifest now Laura?" he asked.

"The Great American novel."

"You're not American."

"I was at school with some people who formed a band. You know what they called it?"

"No."

"Texas. That's what they called it. I'm gonna write the great American novel," I said again. "Who would you like to play you in the film adaptation?" I asked.

"Gerard Depardieu," he said with a laugh.

"Oh come on! The guy's too French!"

"How can you be too French?"

"He can't speak English–can he? Anyway you're way better looking than that. I wouldn't have come all this way for a guy that looked as hoary as Depardieu–he's too old!"

"He's got a vineyard though ... Hey! I didn't think you came on this trip for me ..." he looked over.

"Ford Coppola has a vineyard. He said that making wine was like making a movie. What do you think about that? They all do it these people. They've got so much money, and land and wine never go out of style. You'll never starve if you have a piece of land. Unless you're an Okie but then again, they were tenants, weren't they?"

"You might if you don't look after it," said Leo.

"Did you ever see *The Hangover?* You look like that guy from *The Hangover!*"

"I never heard of it. I've been travelling, remember."

"Four guys go to Vegas on a bachelor party and it becomes a big mess. Someone drops ritalin in their beer," I said.

"You look like the teacher guy with the great pink shades. He's fluent in French in real life, curiously enough."

"You wouldn't have a hangover with a good biodynamic wine. What would the film be called? But then you wouldn't have a film. No sulphur, no story."

"Maybe we'd be a French film. Maybe we'd have a screening at Cannes? It could be called *Les Terroiristes*, all about the quest for wine and love," I said.

"I like it."

"Eventually it would be a long-running musical in the west end. I saw a Claude Sautet film with tons of scenes with wine, groups of men ooh-ing and ahh-ing over crates of wine. I'd no idea French men could bond like this."

"It's a national pastime. I can go anywhere in the world and walk into a wine bar or restaurant or to a vineyard, wherever, and strike up a great friendship over wine. It travels with me everywhere. So who would play you?" he asked.

"You mean the female lead? The gorgeous pouting red-head with a nifty secateur technique and loads of great one liners? It would have to be someone with red hair."

"I love your red hair," said Leo. I was taken aback. "When you were naked in the water. You were really beautiful then."

"I wish men would make more of an effort with their looks," I said. "Some of you look so awful." Did that make me shallow? Beauty was such a power and yet so many ignore it.

"You'll have to make do with me for now."

"You're a natural beauty." I reached over and squeezed his knee.

Three hours later we arrived at The Strip. 'Welcome. Fabulous Las Vegas,' the neon sign said.

60

Vegas was a hell zone. OK so I bought a lottery ticket once in awhile and I like bright lights but this?

Tonight I was a photography widow. The traffic on The Strip was gridlocked so we could stop easily for Leo to lean out of the car window and take pictures. He wanted techno at full volume. I turned the music down. At the wheel again, he turned the volume up once more. We drove down The Strip slowly then stopped and he leaned out and took more photos. I turned the music down again. He said, "You don't like music or what?"

"I don't like rubbish music." I was exhausted.

I watched all those gamblers out there in the street. Stupid modern people. What a cheap town, a junk culture of the worst kind. OK, so I bought a lottery ticket once in awhile but I never won anything.

We wound up at the entrance of The Sahara in an effort to turn around the car. We were stuck. I was fed up stuck in traffic. There was nothing romantic about this–I wanted to escape. I opened the window and looked up at the lights and my gaze fell on the passing crowd and then my eyes fell out of their sockets and I yelled "It's Barry! It's Barry Manilow! It's Barry Manilow! Leo! It's Barry Manilow!"

"Who's Barry Manilow?"

"I have to get out to see him! We have to go and see him! I love Barry Manilow! I can't believe that's Barry Manilow!" Sure, he was dressed down but I knew it was him, I knew it! I opened the door–forgetting passport and money–and ran into the crowd. I ran after him, I tapped him on the shoulder and he turned and it was, it was Barry. He'd had surgery but still, it was him. Barry! "I'm so sorry but I couldn't help myself. I just love *Could It Be Magic?* It's the best pop song ever written. I love you so much." I wanted to drop to my knees, it was like meeting God. "I just wanted to say thank you." Barry broke into a huge grin.

"Thank you," he said.

My heart was aching, the pain and the pleasure of the moment were equal. "God, I love you Barry but I have to go, I've got to get back to the nutter I'm driving with." And so I ran off again. Leo was where I had left him. I wondered if Barry would have looked after me if I'd been stranded.

We drove away from The Strip finally and passed a wedding chapel. I said to Leo, "Will you marry me?"

"No." He turned the car and we were back on The Strip once more. I didn't see Barry again. Maybe I had just imagined meeting him in my desperation. Did that just happen? What was The Universe up to now? I was losing the plot.

As we finally drove out of town, I said, "Did you like Las Vegas?"

"No," he said for the second time that night.

"Neither did I." Our excursion down The Strip lasted one and a half hours in total.

Back over the county line to Arizona some time later, we parked at what seemed like a school building around midnight, the sound of the freeway still within earshot. I had backache from the previous night when I had inadvertently camped on top of a stone in that scary forest. I announced I was going to sleep in the car.

"You never mentioned you had back ache all day. Why do you mention it now?" said Leo.

"I didn't want to drag us down with complaining. I can't pitch my tent here! It's the fucking desert! It's late! I have backache."

"You're lying."

"I'm not lying. I have backache."

Leo got out of the car and started stomping on the sandy verge in front. "You can camp here. There's no problem!" he yelled. There was no way I was pitching my primitive tent or try to in the rocky desert.

I moved to the passenger seat as Leo was settling into the back. "You're in my energy field. It's bad for me. It means you'll be in my energy field all night. You could put your tent up. It's bad for me for you to be in here."

"You and your fucking chakras."

I put in my earplugs and closed my eyes and waited. Sleep would come eventually. I was now practised in sleeping in a car and the thing was not to resist. Not to move and just let the discomfort flow over you. It was multiple discomfort this night with my aching back and as the minutes passed, a bead of sweat dripped from my brow. It was hot. Beads of sweat formed and dripped down my back. I wished for sleep to come but my mind was disturbed. A pain so deep I barely understood. It was loneliness, plain and simple. I was a woman after all, a straight woman. There was a place in my heart for a man.

Certainly, without a love, I felt hindered and hampered. With the wrong person– like now–it was worse. It was rockier territory than the one we'd been driving through.

I still lived in my head too much, slicing reality up with opinions, opinions and beliefs that didn't serve me. Descartes had it all wrong–typical bloody Frenchman. *I am therefore I think.* My mind was a sacred mirror reflecting the All That Is and it was my job to keep that mirror clean. I needed to shift my attention down my body from my head to my heart and live from there. Separation wasn't real, it didn't exist in nature, it existed in my thoughts. I could tune my heart to the Schumann resonance, not the dissonance that was all around me and I could live from there. Dissonance resolved = harmony. Music to my ears.

61

I tread cautiously around Leo in the morning. He wasn't talking. I sorted out my things then sat in the passenger seat waiting. Driving back along the I-93, he took a road turning at a sign, 'Willow Beach 4 miles.' "I wanna swim," he said.

"I could do with the wash too," I replied.

We were alone at the beach and got into the water in underwear. I left him alone as he was swirling around, happy in himself. I ducked under and felt the dust wash off. It was good to be wet. It was good to feel cold. The desert and mountains set me in mind of *Easy Rider*. I remembered the argument I had had with a friend about the ending. Captain America and Billy had blown it. I walked out of the flat that night when he said, "It's a great ending, it's about the sixties!" I said, "No! I want them to go on, they can't be shot dead!" I was younger then and now I had blown it too. My revolutionary moment was soon to be over and what had I achieved?

"Are you feeling better now?" I asked Leo back at the car. The Nepal stove was heating water. "I just wanna get to LA," he said.

"I can brew the coffee if you like?" I prepared us both a cup and leant on the boot of the car. I took a sip. I looked at those mountains. What a morning!

It was true I was at odds with the world but it was the human world I was at odds with. I was complete in myself and the natural environment and I came to it again–it was the world that was mad. For me to adjust would be proof of my insanity, whatever my sisters said. I was a primitive, a nomad and I was happy with that. Earth, Water, Air–oh that clean morning air–and Fire, I was Fire. Fire of life, fire of hope, fire of desire!

We were all alone, it was only us and our lonely Rust Bucket in the Mojave Desert later on the 66. Stopping for a train at a level crossing, I could see how distant the freeway was. No mobile signal and 100 degrees outside. An enormous freight train was thundering along the track, hooting its Air Chime bells in an ecstatic chord, over and over, louder and louder on its approach the na blast of wind and a Doppler shift down a tone as it thundered past, shaking the Rust Bucket and us to our core. "Woo-hoo!" I yelled. 'A' for America–even the trains were musical.

They say technology reduced music to an auditory experience but there were some experiences left that were full bodied ones. This was one of them. Leo and I were in the moment. The industrial revolution had had its compensations, it had been worth it after all. B Major 6th had never sounded so good.

We stopped at a gas station and filled up with water and gas. The mood had switched to survival mode–getting through the drive as opposed to fighting. It had begun to be scary. Those Okies in their thousands with no air conditioning making the journey across the desert, that was epic.

We followed the Oatman Road up and up over the old Route 66. Our guidebook said be careful and The Rust Bucket climbed slowly up and around the narrow road with its sheer drops through the desert, meeting only one other car exactly on top of the mountain at over 3,500 feet at the Sitgreaves Pass. We drove by deserted houses and discarded junk and descended into Oatman, an old cowboy town with stocky *burros* or wild horses walking around in the street, happy as Larry now, left behind after the goldrush.

We made our way back off the mountain and over the desert into lovely California until it was late afternoon and I remembered something Sharon had said, about her love life being like the Mojave Desert, and I reminded Leo, "I was supposed to take the train tonight." So we drove faster.

We were at San Bernardino, on the edge of Los Angeles when the insanity started to take hold. We decided to get off the 66, it was too slow now and too confusing to navigate through eighty miles of city streets. I was never going to make it to Union Station that day so Leo agreed to continue together for Santa Monica, the end of Route 66 but on the freeway. We pressed on. I switched on the radio. French rap. I loved French rap, I liked hearing the French language. I wondered what it was doing on the radio in California. As night fell, it began to rain.

"Do you know we've been driving for over an hour in LA and we're still not at the ocean?" said Leo. We were on the Santa Monica Freeway now.

"OK, let's find a motel? I'll pay. It's time to stop now."

"You always wanna pay for everything."

"No I don't. But I don't mind once in awhile when we need a rest."

"You think money can solve everything. You think you can buy me off."

"It's not like I have that much and I'm happy if it helps us out once in awhile," I said. Placating, grovelling, diminishing and minimising myself–I could hear myself doing it. Jesus!

He continued to drive a faster. "We have to get off the freeway to find somewhere," he said.

"Let's get off then." We were driving faster still, we were chasing our own tails.

"We're gonna get to the ocean first," he replied. "There's something I wanna tell you." He glanced at me. "I'm not single anymore." He pressed his foot on the accelerator.

I looked over at him, his face was hard staring at the rain, his hands gripped on the wheel. His face lit up yellow with blue then red then red again, neon flashing into his eyes. "Two weeks ago I asked her to marry me. Two days ago she said yes."

"I'm sorry?" I looked over at him again, my voice had trawled the depth of my throat unexpectedly with the word sorry and ended with a high note. His eyes were fixed on the road.

He repeated. "I'm not single anymore. I asked her to marry me and two days ago she said yes."

"You're getting married?" My voice retreated to the depths again in my throat and ended up at a higher note. "Where is this woman?!"

"She's back in Canada. I'm gonna drive back when I've finished in California. Up through Oregon to visit some wineries then back into Canada and head east again to see her in Toronto. I've only got three months on my visa in the US and I wanna make the most of it. We're getting married in the fall."

I looked out at the road and the rain and the neon colours flashing past, the rap around my ears. I couldn't comprehend it. Did she know about me? My mind flitted over the last five weeks. I'd had sex with Leo just two days ago. That must have been when she said, 'I do'. I'd been hit over the head with a plank, a Max Planck. The Universe was spinning and my head was too. We drove on.

62

The scales were falling from my eyes. I could feel my upper arms burning, the skin burning off. I looked out at the other cars racing through the night in the rain. I was in a world created by the Powers That Shouldn't Be. Civilisation was based on violence. The violence of the colonisers, the violence meted out to scapegoats and now I realised I was one.

Bankers bust and shafting us, topsoil dead and the biggest oil slick in history pouring into the Gulf of Mexico–the plug was being pulled on the whole shebang. Or was it me? Was I the car crash? If everyone else was seeking redemption in speed and consuming fossil fuels that took the entirety of the earth's existence to create–then it was really a death wish and I may as well join them. But I didn't have a death wish, I had a wish for a rebirth.

I was in the crash. Trapped in his car, I saw that every technology was a form of control. I was being reborn in the USA, in a Canadian Saturn, locked into Stockholm Syndrome with a Frenchman and in a North Korea state of mind. I took the bullshit by the horns. "You told me she was with someone else, you said she was in a relationship with a guy," I said.

"She was. But now she's not."

"Did you have an affair with her when you saw her in Toronto?" I asked.

"Yeah," he said.

"You slept with her behind her boyfriend's back?"

"Yeah, we did," he said.

"Why didn't you tell me?" I asked.

"You didn't ask," he said.

"You've been lying to me all this time?!"

"I've not been lying, I was single until two days ago. I never promised you anything. I always said I didn't want a relationship with you, I've always said that," he said, the self-serving, self-righteous creep.

"We had sex two nights ago, you asked for it. I mean, you started it." I heard that rap from Marseilles, what was it doing on American radio? What was all that about?"

"You wanted it, didn't you?"

"I didn't know you were engaged to be married! You're a liar and a user!"

"You want out of the car now?"

"No," I said.

"What kind of engagement is that, when it's started with an affair behind someone's back and when you get engaged you have sex with someone else? She doesn't even know about me, does she?"

"No."

"How can you trust her when she went behind her boyfriend's back? How can you trust yourself when you've gone behind her back with me?" Jealousy might be the least of it as I felt my confusion and shock rising. "Your plan is flawed."

"I love her and we're gonna get married in the fall. What you gonna do Laura? You don't have a man in your life, you don't have a home, you're late for your train, what you gonna do? You can't even drive. I never wanted a relationship with you. I've always said that. You could come here and do your own trip. You could learn to drive, you can visit wineries on your own. You say you wanted to learn about wine, well that's what you gonna have to do." All my unknown unknowns were now known.

I would never win whilst I was in his car. I occupied a Leo reality, not my own, a reality where you could do just what you liked with other people because they were bystanders on the great drama that was YOU. Besides, I didn't want to be chucked out of the car. I readjusted my seating and stretched my legs further on the floor, my feet now resting on their heels. It was the ejector seat I was sitting in, the rejector seat or, rather, the rejected seat, the seat

I'd been sitting in all my life. I tried to figure out those French rap lyrics and gave up. I lay my head back. I wished the French rappers would shut up.

I no longer believed in past, present and future, cause and effect. I wished to live with the Hopi, in a seamless, timeless realm. Unfortunately, for now I was stuck in the three dimensional plane with an angel-faced trickster. Shiva the Destroyer and Kali, the Goddess of Destruction were out in force.

"We're gonna go and live in Provence. Get a vineyard. She's got some money. I'm gonna make my wine," he said.

"Maybe you'd better auction the wine from your married woman first." I saw a sign that said Santa Monica 5 km. The end of the road was in sight.

63

We drove around Santa Monica for an hour, stopping a couple of times to ask about a room for the night but they were booked or too expensive. Leo parked the car in a quiet street not far from the ocean and said, "OK. I've had enough. We're sleeping here." We could easily get picked up by the police. I was desperate for a pee and got out of the car–with my passport and money just in case he drove away and pulled down my jeans and pants and urinated on the kerb in a backstreet. There's a reason America is the home of the blues.

    I'm so sorry residents of Santa Monica, people of Hollywood and all Americans of good standing. You let me into your lovely libraries to read *The New York Times*, you fed me *huevos rancheros* with red and yellow and blue corn chips, you refilled my coffee as often as I wished and all I've done for you is to pee on the sidewalk. I'm so sorry good people of America. I should never have come. I never wanted a Hollywood career, I never wanted a career full stop period.

    I got into the rejector seat and put on my sleeping mask and earplugs and allowed my mind to drift. The bead of sweat on the brow. The bead of sweat rolling down my back. Sleep was coming. I was aware of the passing of an occasional car. I covered the windscreen and side window as best I could with maps and clothing. I lay my head to the left with two t-shirts on my shoulder as a pillow. I supposed it could be worse. I could be living in Saudi Arabia, or Mexico where they abduct girls and women, or maybe

India where they set fire to them. I twirled my grandmother's wedding ring on my finger. I drifted off.

64

I awoke in the night and checked the car clock. It was 3am, the time between–shit! What the hell was happening? The car was moving! Shit! My God, was it a tremor?

"Leo! Leo! Wake up! Wake up! Leo wake up! Leo!" I reached into the back of the car and there was another tremor as I pulled out his earplug. He hit out at me with his arm.

"What are you doing waking me up. Fuck off!"

"Leo it's an earthquake, we're in an earthquake!"

"Shit! What we gonna do?! Shit!"

It was quiet for a moment until the earth moved again. "Jesus, Leo we better get out of the car. I mean we're in LA, this shit's for real!"

"Maybe we'd better get to the ocean? Let's get out and get to the ocean. Nothing can fall on us there. *Merde*. Should we drive?"

"I dunno–it's not far. I think we better take the car. It's got all our stuff." He came into the driver seat and I changed to the passenger seat. The ocean was two blocks away.

We parked up on the seafront. The waves were enormous, the sky clear and black. There was nobody around. There was no sound of police sirens. It was 3 am after all. The earth seemed stable again. There were a few lights on in houses, the streetlights were working, there were no cracks in the pavement.

"D'you think it was a minor tremor?" I said.

"I dunno."

"How would you find out?" He switched on the radio and twiddled the dial.

"We can't get out, we'll just have to wait it out," he said.

"Maybe it was just a little tremor. First we had the *terroir*, now we've got the tremor."

"I don't wanna die in America."

"Whose stupid idea was it to come to the New World anyhow, there aren't any earthquakes in France."

For once it wasn't my fault, it was the San Andreas fault.

65

It was July 14–Bastille Day, the morning after the quake before. There was no more sleep for us that night so we watched the sun rise over the Pacific as the earth breathed out. Everything seemed as normal on this fine California summer day, this glorious state of California, a good day to see the Pacific for the first time.

My emotions were on bolt down. I cried maybe half a dozen times in those weeks on the road. That might not seem lot to some, but I usually cried just twice a year after adolescence and only because I'd dropped my dinner on the floor the day before my period.

I thought about my mother. Without an inheritance I wouldn't be here. She had set off a strange series of events.

"I can see a tourist office along the road. They're open in fifteen minutes," Leo said. "You wanna come?" I said no. "Maybe you just want to get off now?" he enquired. He knew damn well I didn't know where I was. "No, I don't," I said. "You promised to drop me at the station and you will. I don't know where I am after last night." He put more money in the parking meter and I waited in the car watching the joggers and beach types and vagrants. I was surprised when people were up and busy early in the morning. It continues to surprise me. Leo returned after a few minutes and said, "I want you to come. I want to take a photo."

"You can get anyone to take a photo," I replied.

"I want a photo of both of us," he said. "I wanna go on the pier. There's a sign that's the end of Route 66. I want to get my photo taken so I can show my children."

I walked with him to the pier where I found a cowboy hat at a tourist stall, and some cyclists took a photo of us by the Route 66 sign. It wasn't the one Leo uploaded on his blog. The one on his blog was the sign standing alone. The rim of the cowboy hat had shadowed my face.

We drove to a laundrette afterwards and after I started a wash, I sat on one of the orange plastic seats before a TV hung high on the wall. It was CNN. The oil had been spilling for eighty-six days. Two hundred million gallons of sweet crude, not to mention the millions of gallons of oil dispersant pouring into the Gulf now, on the basis of, 'if you can't see it, it doesn't exist'–like radiation maybe. All that oil now dispersed would act as mini solar panels forever in the ocean in all the world heating up our waters even more. I stared blankly at the images and words. We were being taken advantage of, controlled by our own stupidity, *malbouffe*, rubbish religion and the end result would be a dead planet not a blue one. It's not like they're making more land for us to live on, all that'll be left will be brute force. Consensus reality my ass. I don't give my consent to this consensus. I refuse with a capital R.

The institutions were failing us. Bankers and politicians couldn't fix anything for me nor for anyone else. Come to think of it, neither could Jimmy Saville. I was going to have to fix things for myself. No wonder I'd been floundering. No wonder the powers that shouldn't be wanted media control. No wonder they wanted to put the squeeze on a poor person. No wonder science had been co-opted to the one view, the only view, this scientific view.

You could be religious, OK, but no-one would take you seriously. Reason with a capital R had been running the show but I preferred R for Revolutionary, I say R is for Refusal. Slowly but surely the wheel would turn, the one view wasn't the only view on the event horizon. You were fooled to thinking that this was inevitable, this one view, that we'd lived like this forever, but you'd be wrong. What if the self doesn't end with the ego? What if your inner nature was the real truth? What then? Did you breathe with your ego? Did you make your heart beat? No. It happened of its own volition, a power both in you and without you, doing it for you and to you. Ignore those politicians, they were *matterhead* power dogs of the technocracy. And if you want to live in a *matterhead* technocracy, then you're dead already. Didn't I use to be Laura McLove? We didn't need a spiritual evolution, it was spiritual revolution that was called for, a revolution in *f e e l i n g*. Revolution with a capital R, one that the Powers That Shouldn't Be would ever get their oil soaked hands on. I was a living breathing fucking heartbeating processing affair, not fixed, I was free.

I was in full on megadoomer mode now, in the throes of a grand *mal du siecle* and decided on coffee and a sandwich from the Subway next door to settle my nerves. I returned to my seat. I watched Leo from the corner of my eye as he took out his clothes and stuffed them in a machine. He was wearing a long beige Nepal shirt with side slits at the thighs and those cotton pickin' hemp pants, now filthy. The shirt came to his knees. Glancing back and forth to the TV, I continued to watch with amusement while he proceeded to take off his trousers, then his boxer shorts and put them in the machine. He was now dressed only in the long shirt, exposing the side of his thighs, and a pair of $1 flip flops from *Family Dollar*. He was *sans culottes*. All Nepal, no knickers.

The Mexican laundromat worker strode up to him, mop in hand and shouted, "I'll call the police! You can't be in here naked! There are women in here!"

"I've got clothes on, what's the problem?" said Leo.

"There are women in here. You can't dress like that, it's against the law."

Leo removed his filthy trousers from the machine and put them on again. "See? happy now?" he said to the old Mexican guy. No wonder I had had such conflicts with him on the road. He had conflicts with everyone–the police, the laundry guy, me–well, that was the line up. He's French, I wanted to say, he can't help himself. I remained quiet and watched the TV. Leo somehow then began to chat to the Mexican attendant. They were now becoming best of friends.

Next stop: Hollywood. We rode back into town on the Santa Monica Boulevard until we took a left onto Sunset and slowed through the McDonald's drive-in for Leo to have a burger and a burger chaser. He was hungry in Hollywood, I was a Hollywood has bean-burger. Leo resumed his fuming–it was the worst ever, the worst since the first night in Long Island. First the *terroir*, then the tremor, now the Terror. Our relationship had reached its radical phase. These French guys knew their intimate *terroir*.

"What you gonna do Laura? When you get back to England. What you gonna do? You gonna find a man to look after you? You wanna find out about wine? You can find out about wine. You wanna take a car trip? Why don't you learn to drive? Why are you here anyway? What you gonna manifest now with your tricks? You think you're gonna be a writer–you can't even get that right. Who are you anyhow? You think you're so great but I like people who've got passion. You don't have any passion. I mean what do you really like?"

"I like *Sex and The City*."

I was still a woman in search of a story but now I'd found my genre. On Sunset Boulevard, I was a character, driven, and I'd settle for melodrama. I knew never to judge a man until you had walked in his moccasins for two moons but five weeks in the passenger seat, it was time for my review. We took another turning this time onto Hollywood Boulevard and drove slow to see the Hollywood sign in the hills.

The trouble with the French is that they hadn't created *film noir* and now my past was coming back to haunt me. As a wine needs expression so my writing needed a voice and passing the Kodak Theatre, I gave it my best performance. In a world of sellouts and remakes, I wrote my own Hollywood ending. "Jesus Leo. What's the matter with you? It's supposed to be a vagina and an attitude in this town that's lethal. Is that the problem? Do you have vagina envy? By the way I AM great, it's this story that's got too small. And Laura McLove? *C'est moi*."

Next we were on the 101. As above, so below–as within, so without–and I saw CARS. California dreamin'? More like California nightmare. I had never experienced so much traffic in my life. It was a cancer. What had happened to America? Was there no more rockin' in the free world? America had changed but I hadn't. I was a child of the sixties. I wanted the America of Whitman and Melville, Ginsberg and Kerouac, Bukowski and Fante. Breadheads, *matterheads*, your time is up! The revolutionary wheel will turn once more, a butterfly will flap its wings and at last, the meek shall inherit the earth. It was time to evolve and the time was NOW. I could be the World Dancer with the revolution at my feet instead of trapped inside the wheel. It was love that moved Phil Connors out of *Groundhog Day* and it would be love, a lovely revolution, a resonant entrainment, a collective journey from the head to the heart that would save us.

On my map it looked like forever to get to Union Station but then I saw the sign. "It's our turning!" I yelled. Five minutes later we parked outside the train station. I hauled out my stuff and left a few things behind for Leo to sort which he, of course, complained about.

We said our goodbyes and hugged. A single tear rolled down my cheek and I felt a pang in my solar plexus. That bubble floated up once more in my mind's eye and in that bubble was written the word 'Love.' All you need is love. That was all I needed. Older now, I recognised it for the trick it was and I turned away from Leo and the car and walked towards the station.

It was the last time I saw him.

66

I didn't throw myself under a train at the station, I did what I always did and bought myself a coffee. I shook my head as I took the first sip–I'd just spent the night in a car with a nutter in an earthquake. I was angry at myself too but mostly I was sad. My quest for love had failed and I would not, could not, make that quest again. I'd blown it.

A black woman seated two tables away called over to me and said, "I like your hair!" She introduced herself as Cleopatra. She was seventy years old, she said and somehow we began talking about Watts and the race riots and how they used to keep chickens and grow their own food. I told her about biodynamics and planting by the moon. She then revealed something else. She said, "I had an opening to Spirit when I was nineteen and I could talk to the plants."

"Really?"

"Yes, it's gone now mostly but for a couple of years there I really could sense it. So what are you going to do when you finish your trip?"

"I'm going to live in England," I replied.

"No," she said. "You're going to live here."

"I can't imagine that." I had lost all sense of myself in America, it was so huge.

"You will come to live here." She was adamant. I shook inside, just like the earth had shaken me last night. She said, "I shook inside when I said that."

"So did I."

I took the train up the coastal route to San Francisco and visited The Haight and the City Lights bookstore. It was then I noticed Leo had defriended me on Facebook. Our relationship was officially *terminé*–over. So was my trip. I had no heart for it left, no heart for America.

The coming of Leo Vigneron had been the beginning and end of my life on the road. Leo Vigneron had been the worst guy for the road because he was a rugged individualist with major mother issues. I thought of Leo Vigneron, his flaxen hair, his Hollywood looks, I thought of Leo Vigneron tasting wine, driving like a maniac, his ideas, his accent, his magnificent penis. Yes, Leo Vigneron was on my mind, the longing gone at last. I knew what lay inside him and it wasn't great. It wasn't even good.

Still confused, manless, jobless, rudderless and homeless, I clicked my boots three times and booked a flight back to London. I got my period the day I returned and I knew I'd started menopause.

A friend came to meet me at the airport and I said to her, "I think I may write a novel." So I wrote this like life depended on it, which it did.

I thought of vineyard soil–alive, but poor for the vine to struggle and express its sweetness in the grapes. Then I said, "I think I may write a song too."

My thoughts turned to Barry and the best pop song ever written.

It could be magic.

♪ ♪ *The End* ♪ ♪

ABOUT THE AUTHOR

Claire Doyle is a musician turned writer. She lives in Hungary where she wrote her second novel, The Budapest Artists' Club. When Claire Doyle isn't writing or going for a walk, she can be found trying to learn Hungarian folk dancing. Or trying to speak Hungarian. Sometimes both at the same time. Claire Doyle lives in Budapest's party quarter.

ALSO BY CLAIRE DOYLE

The Budapest Artists' Club
A Novel

Music. Dance. Betrayal. Budapest, 1999. Millennium Night. Two identical violas. An instrument 'heist'. But for what? What is the mystery of the strange three-stringed viola that has been hanging in a Romanian museum for decades? A walk through the past for Laura McLove as she returns to present day Budapest, in search of a folk dancer called Zoltán, all the while retelling the strange tale when she became the fall girl for a musical instrument heist in those inbetween days–post communism, pre EU. *Those Were The Days* ... Will she find Zoltán? And what's with the three strings anyway?

A little bit retro, a little bit rock 'n' roll. Come and join Laura and her old friend Valentin as they once again go dancing at The Budapest Artists' Club. You're never too old to fancie a folkie.

Hungarian Folk Dancing For Beginners
A Short Story

Traditional rites from a Friday night. A downtown love story, with love from Budapest.

♫ ♫ ♫ ♫ ♫ ♫

COPYRIGHT

The Naked Sommelier © 2018 Claire Doyle May 2018
First published under the title "Mother Road" in 2015

ALL RIGHTS RESERVED.

No part of this book publication may be reproduced, stored in a retrieval system, or transmitted in any form or by any means - electronic, mechanical, photocopy, recording or any other - except brief quotation in reviews, without the prior permission of the author.

Note: This is a work of fiction. Names, characters, places, and incidents are a product of the author's imagination. Locales and public names are sometimes used for atmospheric purposes. Any resemblance to actual people, living or dead, or to businesses, companies, events, institutions, or locales is completely coincidental.

Printed in Great Britain
by Amazon